You Don't Need Four Women
to Play Shakespeare

You Don't Need Four Women to Play Shakespeare

Bias in Contemporary American Theatre

by
Ida Prosky

McFarland & Company, Inc., Publishers
Jefferson, North Carolina, and London

British Library Cataloguing-in-Publication data are available

Library of Congress Cataloguing-in-Publication Data

Prosky, Ida, 1935–
   You don't need four women to play Shakespeare : bias in
contemporary American theatre / by Ida Prosky.
     p. cm.
   Includes bibliographical references and index.
   ISBN 0-89950-729-8 (lib. bdg. : 55# alk. paper) ∞
   1. Theatre – United States – Casting. 2. Women in the theater –
United States. 3. Sex discrimination against women – United States.
4. Theater and society – United States. I. Title.
PN2293.C38P76 1992
792′.028′082 – dc20   92-7310
                                                          CIP

Manufactured in the United States of America

McFarland & Company, Inc., Publishers
  Box 611, Jefferson, North Carolina 28640

TABLE OF CONTENTS

Preface   vii

One. You Don't Need Four Women to Play
          Shakespeare   1

Two. Lower Pay, Less Voice Hurt the Status
          of Women   29

Three. Stepping into the Aura   45

Four. Investing in the Group and Owning the Work   61

Five. They Don't Call It Show Art   77

Six. Making a Life Outside the Theater   103

Seven. But What Do You Really Do?   121

Eight. Another Look in the Mirror: Future, Past,
          and Perspective   137

Bibliography   155

Index   157

PREFACE

There is a growing body of literature in anthropology that focuses on the performing arts: Richard Schechner's cross-cultural work in theater, Victor Turner's examination of the nature of performance, Judith Hanna on sexuality and gender roles in dance. These works have been most helpful in developing a theoretical perspective for my own interest in the performer and the distinctive patterns of interaction between life and work that characterize actors and actresses and set them apart as a special group within society.

In *The Anthropology of Performance*, Victor Turner examines the art of performance and the various meanings of the word *play*. One of the meanings is that play is done in the subjunctive mood. It expresses a contingent or a hypothetical action. "It is concerned with supposition, conjecture, and assumption, with the domain of as if rather than as is" (Turner 1986, 169).

In *The Empty Space*, Peter Brook makes a similar observation and remarks upon the range of creative possibility inherent in this type of thinking.

In everyday life, "if" is a fiction, in the theatre "if" is an experiment. In everyday life, "if" is an evasion, in the theatre "if" is the truth. When we are persuaded to believe in this truth, then the theatre and life are one. This is a high aim. It sounds like hard work. To play needs much work. But when we experience the work as play, then it is not work anymore. A play is play [Brook 1968, 141].

Women and men in the theater use this element of the range of possibility for exploration and transformation as part of their tools of their profession. They form a special group distinguished by the "play" element of their profession as well as by the different routine of their working lives. In the United States, where government subsidies for theater are limited, actors and actresses also come to terms with the practical business of making a living in a culture that does not give them very much help. This necessary combination of creativity and economic survival skills also distinguishes American actors from those who work in countries where theater is subsidized. An older actor says there have been times when the intellectual, emotional, and physical demands of his profession gave direction and structure to his life outside the theater, and other times when his life offstage began to inform and enrich his work on stage. It is this interaction between life and work that my research attempts to examine.

Gender Bias in the Theater

In her review of feminist anthropology, Henrietta Moore describes the study of gender, which concerns itself with "the interrelations between women and men, and the role of gender in structuring human societies" (Moore 1988, 6). She writes (page 196) that "forms of difference in human social life – gender, class, race, culture, history, etc. are always experienced, constructed, and mediated in interrelation with each other." That concept has been helpful in organizing data on multiple forms of bias (gender, age, race) which affect women in the theater.

Whether performers are focused on their own creative process or feel a deep connection to the production as a whole, theater is generally an area where men and women work together. There can be enormous ego problems, but it is still a profession where those involved in it find it possible to say "the basis of respect is in the work." That attitude often tempers working relationships. Although my research deals more specifically with the problems of women, I have used both men and women as informants because I feel that to exclude men would not provide an adequate description of the ways in which actors and actresses experience success and difficulty in pursuing their work.

This book grew out of two research projects which I did with performers working in Washington over the past five years. Both of these projects examined the extent and forms of gender bias that operates in different ways against both sexes in the theater, but particularly against women. Beyond the fact that many more parts are written for men, the effect of this problem on women is eloquently described by a Black actress who is only in her thirties.

At a certain point . . . you begin to feel you've become invisible, or
you leap from playing the young mother to the grandmother. Where
is the play that speaks to my experience of everything in between.
It's a big wasteland in which you feel unimportant. For men, there's
a steady continuum of available roles. They're not stereotyped as
heavily as women. Consciously or not, you begin to feel valueless
after a certain age. I go to the movies and never see myself. There
is no one like me. That's why I create my own work, to speak to my
own experience and other women like me.

This problem of the lack of roles has to do with the way plays are
written, but also with traditional casting choices and the range of
plays that theaters include in their regular seasons. The challenge of
fewer roles that women face when they choose to work in the theater
is increased by a deficit in the size and quality of those roles across
a wide age range.

As the actress's comment indicates, this can affect the way
women on stage and women in the audience value or devalue their
self-image as they mature. To address this problem, she suggests an
active strategy that a number of women and minority performers of
both sexes have chosen in recent years. By creating their own work
and establishing companies, they generate opportunities to develop
a stronger public voice for themselves and others like them. Some
of this work eventually makes its way into mainstream theater,
films, and television where it informs and reminds us of the true
diversity of our experience.

This research is based on 50 structured interviews with actors,
actresses, directors, and stage managers who range in age from 19
to 78. The interviews were supplemented by information gathered
from a survey specifically directed to the question of gender bias
which was mailed to a stratified random sample of 244 performers
drawn from a population of 735 performers who worked in the
theater in Washington from May 1986 to May 1987. Background
observations also come from innumerable visits to theaters, film and
television location sites, and casual talks with theater people over
the past several years.

Since interviews cover a wide age range, there is some historical
perspective on how changes in the theater have affected performers'
lives over the past 40 or so years. Young actresses come to the
theater today with more education and training but face greater
competition. Those interviewed here assume that they are entitled
to a more equal footing with men and they are not easily intimidated

by authority. Americans as a group have always been less patient with received wisdom than with what they can discover for themselves. This cultural trait, which in recent years can be more openly expressed by women, wars against certain elements of theatrical tradition. It creates an undercurrent of tension between the performer at the bottom and the producer and director at the top of a hierarchy of power structures in the theater.

In the course of interviews, other cultural, historical, and economic elements of gender bias emerged that constrain men who choose acting as a career. Societal attitudes towards men in the arts are not often examined in the general press and are not always understood. For example, an article in a recent national news magazine examined possible explanations for the fact that few male ballet dancers are being trained in this country. It did so without ever mentioning that dancers as a group are even more poorly paid than actors and, as members of a company, may have short careers and even more itinerant lives. Given these conditions, it is no surprise that many American men do not choose dance as a career. Men who choose acting have somewhat similar problems. Because gender bias against men takes a form strikingly different from bias against women, it is included here in a separate chapter.

Since not everyone I talked to agreed that there is bias against either sex in the theater, it seemed important to present a full range of opinion. One of the best descriptions of how hard a taskmaster the theater can be for everyone comes from an older actor who was listening to a group of apprentices air their legitimate complaints. "Of course it's not fair," he said. "If you want 'fair,' join the civil service." With that in mind, I have tried to present a dialogue between the many different people who talked to me. The rigorous demands that theater makes on both men and women is the basic argument for a central idea of this work: that it is in the challenge of performance that women learn to craft a more effective voice for themselves in their work. When that experience is powerful enough, it can also be a mechanism for growth in their personal lives as well.

Although many of these interviews were conducted while the performers were working in Washington, work situations described occurred in locations as diverse as Denver, Chicago, San Francisco, New York, or on a film set in eastern Tennessee. Mobility is a major requirement for working in the American theater. Since the 1950s, regional theater has created jobs for actors all over the country and in recent years, the League of Regional Theaters contract has generated more work for actors than Broadway houses (*Equity News* 1988). So while it is possible to talk about a Washington theater community, the realities of competing for a limited number of paying jobs in any one location means that most actors try to work in as many different media as they can and be ready to go wherever jobs are available.

Informant Anonymity

A distinguishing feature of anthropology that works as a safeguard for those who contribute their ideas and opinions toward an ethnography is the principle of informant anonymity. By this, I mean that no individual's name is ever attached to his or her comments and that the circumstances of an individual's identity will be disguised if the nature of their comments makes it appropriate. Paul Espinosa, in his doctoral dissertation on "Text-Building in a Hollywood Television Series," describes the increased level of accountability "affecting both sides of the fieldwork bond" in the study of a powerful community.

There are a number of reasons why this anonymity is particularly important to performers. Jobs often depend upon a carefully developed network of personal and professional associations. Any direct criticism of management procedures or artistic decisions can endanger that job network. Performers who are in the habit of protecting their work associations may feel that they are guarding their professional reputation as well. As one informant put it "actors have no job protection. Part of an actor's reputation depends on how well he gets along with other people."

For actresses of any age, it is clear that concealing one's real age is not an act of vanity but a matter of professional self-preservation. Even women in their twenties and thirties say that they never fill in age blanks on employment forms. Since part of this research deals with questions of age bias against women, preserving the confidentiality of information on the age of specific individuals is particularly important.

With this in mind, I cannot thank by name the men and women I interviewed and those who responded to the survey and so I thank them generally for their generosity, passionate commitment to their profession, and insightful comments. They are an articulate group of people accustomed to analyzing their situation and their response to it. They are creative people who have to deal with an extremely difficult economic situation. Making a living in the theater often translates into holding several jobs on a daily basis. This was true of many of the younger performers I interviewed. Sometimes one job in the theater can be so demanding that it might as well be three. One actress came for an interview between the dentist, the doctor, and rehearsal for a five-day tour of Israel. As a group they were generous not only with their time but in sharing information with me on their lives in the theater. Even in discussing what were obviously difficult situations, performers appeared to make careful assessments of what happened and to be fair to the individuals or institutions involved. Washington in particular enjoys quality theater largely because of the creativity, skill, and commitment of the performers who work there.

My husband, Robert, has been an invaluable source of contacts, information, and encouragement for this study. My interest in the theater began at the age of seven when I saw *Arsenic and Old Lace* at the National Theater. My knowledge of how actors and actresses live and work comes from 30 years of marriage to an actor. For more than 20 of those years, while Bob was a member of the resident company at Arena Stage, I saw both the final productions and a great deal of the working process that went into them. The routine of our daily lives revolved around the schedule of the theater. He has since worked in New York, Chicago, and wherever film and television projects take him. But I know that he feels that his acting abilities were largely formed in those years at Arena. My own expectations of the function theater should serve in people's lives also comes from that experience. When David Mamet speaks of the phenomenal strength and generosity of the actor, I think of the actors and actresses I have known and I understand what he means. I think particularly of Bob. He has been a tremendous help in this research.

ONE

YOU DON'T NEED FOUR WOMEN TO PLAY SHAKESPEARE

When I first began to interview men and women who work in the theater, an actor told me the following story. He was working with a small Shakespeare festival that he said had made "the God-awful mistake of hiring four women for their season." They were having a terrible time on their limited budget, trying to find enough parts in the plays they had chosen to keep all four actresses employed. He put the mistake down to their lack of familiarity with the playwright. He felt that anyone who has done a lot of Shakespeare would know that "you don't need four women to play Shakespeare. You need a young one, an old one, and someone who's willing to play the maid."

Aside from the fact that stereotypes in casting can be just that absurd, his story illustrates a central difficulty for women who choose to work on stage. Throughout the classical literature of the theater (those plays that have become the benchmarks of the actor's abilities) and in modern plays up to recent years, there have always been more parts written for men than for women.

Performers, both men and women, offer various explanations for this problem. An actor links the bias in the literature to "prevailing" attitudes in the culture.

Theater is a mirror of society. It is the result of prevailing societal prejudices that men's problems and concerns are simply more inter-

1

esting than women's. Or that if women's concerns are looked at, they're always in relation to men. . . . I don't think it's specific to the theater. I think it mirrors more general historical perspectives. If you want to write a historical play, all you've got are records of men. Unless you take a flight of fancy, you're going to end up dealing with men's actions and thoughts historically and currently as well.

Another actor takes a different view of the social realities he sees in the world around him. "There are many dynamic women's roles in society that are rarely portrayed in theater. I don't know why."

An actress addresses the problem in terms of what general audiences want to see. This may or may not affect individual playwrights, but it certainly has an influence on the types of plays that are produced commercially and perhaps experimentally as well.

I think that men are afraid [of looking closely at how women are changing] because before they had women in the palm of their hand. Women were the weaker sex. Men are beginning to [accept change] now, but I don't think they really want to see that. Truthfully, they are afraid of that because their position is lessened. . . . I think probably that's why there aren't roles for women yet. Men don't want to see that.

An actress comments on how this bias is evolving in the current literature of the theater and in contemporary society.

Plays are so often written about people in power, people in leadership positions, people doing important things. Now that women are infiltrating all segments of society, there will be an evening out of the number of male/female roles. [Meanwhile] we've got however many centuries of dramatic literature with kings and dukes in the spotlight. This evening out will take time.

An actress who is also a playwright comments on the minimal rate of change evident in the New York theater. "In the Dramatists Guild, when we go to meetings, there's me and Betty Comden, and Wendy Wasserstein and Ruth Goetz and about a dozen others to fifty or sixty men." Having begun her career in the 1930s, she also points out how the importance of female stars lessened as the portrayal of women in plays changed over a critical period of time.

When I started, all the big stars were women, Katharine Cornell, Jane Cowl, Helen Hayes. Somehow that's altered. I think it's stupid of producers. They should make some women stars.

Franchelle Stewart Dorn as Lady Macbeth. Photographer: Joan Marcus. Courtesy of Shakespeare Theatre at the Folger.

Plays changed. There was a period when what you might call the kitchen sink play was going on, after Osborne's *Look Back in Anger* made such a hit. Women were bedraggled and in the kitchen. They weren't glamorous-looking creatures. Also the wonderful authors who could write comedy, Noel Coward, Philip Barry, Robert Sherwood, died off and writing comedy, upper-class comedy, isn't done too often. They don't call for women stars, the plays today.

Another actress compares the advancement of women into pivotal roles in the work place and the representation of women in powerful leadership positions in the theater. She suggests that the transient nature of the work and the portrayal of women in plays contributes to the female performer's lack of status.

Women don't get tracked into technical or producing or directing roles early on. To the degree that women traditionally have been tracked away from technical and leadership roles, this absolutely reflects a societal bias. But there is also a special bias in theater, which is allowed to persist because there is rarely a clear path along which one progresses. In a business, for example, one goes through a series of career benchmarks, either in a very defined way like the steps in a union or government [job] or through incremental increases in salary, title, etc. Thus, they have a way to push people up into positions of more authority and security.

In the theater, actors, directors, playwrights and technicians move from job to job, except in the rare instances where a company exists. Because you start from a new place with each job, those with power tend to have their power reenforced, and those with less power have a powerlessness reenforced. ... I think this tends to keep women in a more beholden status than in the real world.

The actual roles that are written for women typically are less powerful in substance and style than those for men. I've found that what a role carries with it tends to influence the way a production relates to the actors. I'm always happier with myself and the way others treat me if I'm in a strong role. ... when the roles are for characters who are more easily dismissed, the actress herself may be more easily dismissed, in my experience.

Speaking from her own experience in both the business world and in theater, she suggests that there are mechanisms at work in the latter which tend to maintain the status quo with regard to the advancement of women. Whether the transience of the performers' work operates only against women or against men as well is probably a matter of degree. Both women and men agree that performers are relatively powerless people in the hierarchy of commercial theater. However, these mechanisms associated with the "business" as opposed to the artistry of performance can be crucial for actresses since it is in negotiating with the "business" end of theater that performers make their livelihood. I have only anecdotal evidence that women are paid less than men for stage work but in the more affluent work of films and television, union statistics indicate that women make less money than men.

The cultural construction of gender which equates male/female with public/domestic underlies the playwright's point of view in much of what is written for the stage according to an actor. "As soon as you want to write a play that doesn't take place in someone's residence, there's going to be more men visible." Whether or not this statement accurately represents contemporary American life is less to the point than whether or not many playwrights (and actors) believe that it does.

It is a paradox that as society in this country becomes more diverse, the representation of that society in dramatic literature appears more and more limited to some performers. A Black actress talks about how this narrow view affects her and what it means in terms of educating and nurturing a Black theater-going audience.

I can't see that my circumstances or the circumstances of the women I interact with have been deeply examined. You can go to the theater and see what's happening to men. You can see that examined on a certain level. I don't see myself. I have to come out talking about some other aspect of the play. But I don't come out talking about myself and realizing something about myself that I can go home and grapple with and come to some sort of change as a result of.

In the work I have committed my life to, I should be able to say every once in a while, that I have been able to look at myself more deeply. Even in a large part of Black theater, I see that as Black playwrights try to feed more and more into the mainstream there are only certain aspects of Black life that they examine. So the complexities of being a woman, of being Black, of being a Black woman are almost never examined. And you're left with having to examine aspects of life other than your own.

I think theater should have a commitment to say who is sitting in front and give some time to everyone so that people really can be educated and transformed when they come here. What happens for us as women is that after a while you stop even demanding that. You see so little that you just stop expecting it anyway . . . or you get all excited because you're surprised that someone really said something that meant something to you. I think it's tragic. I think it's something that people should get angrier about.

But a large part of the population doesn't even consider theater as something that is going to impact on their lives. So why get too upset about it. Forget it. Theater doesn't have anything to do with me. And never does. And never will.

The "complexities of being a woman, of being Black, of being a Black woman" is an apt description of the multiple layers of experience that remain largely unexamined in contemporary theater. The idea that theater should have room for a social conscience in relation to performers and to the changing nature of society is at odds with theater as a viable business concerned with selling tickets and entertaining audiences. Yet it continues to surface in letters to *Equity News* which often acts as a forum for arguments on either side. Although most performers agree that there are more parts for men than for women, many do not see this as a form of bias. "Playwrights and screenwriters don't write to employ actors. They write to tell a story. You work as an actor in jobs that you're perfect for – age, sex, size, etc. It's a necessarily discriminatory profession."

The imbalance in roles is familiar to anyone who has been going to the theater for forty-some years but it was also something that I had not consciously noted. Recently, I began to count the number of parts in productions in Washington – *The Tempest*, 10 men, 1 woman; *Juno and the Paycock*, 13 men, 6 women – and in New York – *Arsenic and Old Lace*, 10 men, 3 women; *Devil's Disciple*, 10 men, 5 women. These numbers suggest the extent of gender bias in the older literature of the theater. I wonder how many young women applying to professional training programs in universities are aware of that imbalance.

A look at newer plays shows that the male/female ratio is more evenly divided but, since casts are usually smaller, the number of roles for women has not actually increased. In spite of this imbalance, most of the actors and actresses interviewed noted the predominance of women at auditions and in classes. When asked to estimate the most competitive age range for women, most performers chose the years from 20 to 30. An agent suggests that those who begin their careers before they are 20 have a competitive edge. An actor says, "An interesting thing I note when teaching is that women outnumber men taking classes and often outnumber the men in quality and in talent which is depressing. There are too many good women and too few roles." Given this situation, why are there so many young women choosing to try to work in the theater?

Among the many possible answers to that question may be the attraction of two diverse elements: risk and control. In discussing their professional lives and the ways in which their work has shaped their personal lives, control and risk are often cited as significant motivating forces by the women interviewed here. In complex and sometimes conflicting ways, performers associate these two elements with the creative process. This is as true for the 22-year-old working to understand the shifting demands of a soap opera script on her seventh call-back, as it is for the 50-year-old putting together the production money for a one-woman show in Scandinavia.

Some people who have spent a very long life in the theater realize they do not understand it completely themselves. The image of a child learning how to command attention occurs to several older theater women. One of them says, "It's a risky business to go on the stage. That's what you ask yourself: why am I doing this? I was crazy for attention . . . From a little girl, I was a show-off. I would get up and play the piano for people and I couldn't even play the piano. It's an ego-bolstering thing that acting gives you." A young actress just out of school, describes how she tried for several years not to choose a career in acting but finally found that she was having more trouble avoiding it.

> Most of my friends had neat little packages of lives. They had gone straight through school and were working . . . for me it was a wandering period. . . . I tried everything I could think of besides acting. . . . It became clearer and clearer that I was going to have to give it a try. If it's as hard as everyone says it is, it was harder for me to avoid it.

Young people who do begin to work as adults in professional theater risk losing the normal experience of their high school years and the last part of their childhood. A 17-year-old who spent a year in a resident company before she finished high school talks about what she learned about the profession and what she learned about herself.

> More than anything that year gave me a sense of what it's like to work in theater, not act. I grew up at the [theater] kind of. It started becoming an unconscious value that I'd rather go to rehearsal than to a party. . . . It's something I wasn't very conscious of and then on my graduation night I did [the play] and I realized how much I was missing. So I grew up too fast. It's hard now realizing that I skipped

a lot along the way. It probably always will be [hard] because theater will always be more important than going to a party. Somewhere in the back of my mind, I'd much rather work.

The attraction for her was not adulation. Cast in small roles, she was always aware that applause was never just for her and it was clear to her from her classmates' comments when they came to see her perform that they had little understanding of the focus and discipline of the work and what it meant to her to be part of that theater company. The attraction for her seems to be in the energy and commitment of the group concentrated on the making of the play.

To others, the creative process itself is the challenge. An actress describes the attraction she finds in the continually changing aspect of that process. Theater for her provides both impetus and focus for self exploration. It forces confrontation with inner fears and doubts. In that it requires the interaction of performers, playwright, director, and audience, the creative process of theater widens the world of "self," establishing connections between the individual and the group level of experience.

> I'm one of those people who's always trying to recreate the meaning of life. I never stop reforming meaning so I'm constantly striving to improve and change and alter what I have at the present moment. And that keeps me moving and trying different things. To me the theater has always been the biggest challenge. I've always felt it's the most difficult thing I could have chosen to have done. A lot of things would have been easier for me . . . I really have to stretch myself as hard as I can to do theater.
>
> It's the ultimate challenge partly because it hits all kinds of passions and desires that I have. It also confronts my fears and the negative side of my life, my innate personality, my ingrowth. It forces me to deal with them. There's a lot of value in it [that] I keep rediscovering. I'm finding new areas of value that go beyond myself.

In the sense that continual, nonjudgmental learning is required of performers throughout their working lives, there is an agelessness to the profession. A woman director comments on the general perception of most people that they will have acquired their working knowledge of the world by the time they are well established in their professional and their family lives. They are in a sense "finished" people. She points out that actors tend to be "completed as a human being much later, to be less rigid, more alive in the moment." For both men and women, the creative process of theater calls upon the performer to be open to a continual exploration of the self and the world with a very specific focus. A beginning actor describes a rehearsal experience that is formative in his life as well as his work.

It suddenly struck me what I was doing. I found myself able to do what any actor will tell you you're supposed to do. I was separating each phrase. Every phrase had a purpose and I found I was able to manipulate that purpose and very subtly change the whole sense of the speech . . . not just say it believably but to effect a change in the people to whom I was talking. It's so fundamental but it was organic, not intellectual.

During that period, one night I listened to Mozart and it suddenly made sense to me, the effectiveness I had achieved in exploiting behavior in each phrase. I realized that Mozart was doing the same thing. For a moment, I felt I had had a glimpse of something basically human [regarding] variety and specificity, and the germ of those two things had to do with the question why. One of the basic properties of the artistic process and also of living your life is the constant asking of the question why. As soon as an answer is ascertained, you suddenly have a new question.

I realized there were levels of participation in the life process that I was completely oblivious to.

There are possibilities inherent in the nature of performance. In spite of the structure and discipline of stagecraft, that nature is ephemeral. The life of the play exists only in the moment between these performers and this audience. Like any hand-crafted thing, none of these three (play, performers, audience) will ever come together in exactly the same way again. An older actress explains her fascination with this aspect of performance.

I love the rehearsal process of exploring and finding things and interacting. . . . Then there is a routine that settles in when you get into performance. You go in, you do something every night that's the same. You put your make-up on the same, you do your exercises, and then you go out into this space and anything can happen. There's a structure before and after with this period in between where anything can happen.

These comments describe some of the ways in which performers are drawn to the freedom to explore ideas and emotions in a rehearsal situation where judgment is temporarily suspended. It is a powerful experience to be able to focus and control energy while stepping into the heightened life of the play where characters confront and struggle with each other. The risks undertaken are imaginary but because of the nature of performance they are experienced as real. Pulses pound, muscles tense, and life moves out of the ordinary. I asked one of my sons if he had lost his mind one fall when he got himself into three plays while he was finishing high school, taking SAT exams, and applying to colleges. He said he only felt really alive when he was in performance.

An actor friend reminds me that control and risk are also two basic elements of dramatic conflict that move the characters through whatever transformation or change is called for in a play. They are, in a sense, enabling factors or doorways to other possibilities, other solutions. This idea may have special resonance for women. A director comments, "If being an actress is about an active imagination and the possibility of transforming, it may be that it's an outlet for getting out of the box of being brought up as a woman and feeling certain pressures within the society that seek to define women in a subservient or limiting role."

Many changes both in society and in the structure of theater in this country have made the profession more accessible to women. Greater freedom of choice and increasing job opportunities are now available to women in American society. Since the feminist movement of the 1960s, both the status of women and their role in society have come up for examination in the public consciousness. From necessity or choice, large numbers of women at many different levels of society have redefined their role from primarily wife and mother to wage-earner outside the home as well as wife and mother. The professions still most readily available to women, teaching, nursing, social work, secretarial, assume that these areas of work are best suited to the inherent nurturing abilities of women. What distinguishes women who chose to work in theater is that, in the view of men who work with them, they cannot afford to exercise the nurturing abilities they are assumed to have because of the elements of competition and conflict inherent in the profession. A young director who understands and respects the performer's creative process says

> I think that the women who work in the theater are not allowed to play a maternal nurturing role as they relate to other artists because in order to survive, they have to develop a creative aggression, just to be actively creative, because acting is so much about

conflict within a given set of circumstances. If you're going to play the game, you're going to have to play it with a certain volition or you're going to lose. Actresses . . . are perceived mostly by men in the theater like the young female executive: a woman who is an actress is a tough woman.

Women who chose acting as a career violate the cultural expectation that women should be passive, quiet, undemanding, avoiding or diffusing confrontation, complimentary in the sense that they see their role as fitting around that of a man. Perhaps actresses have always been women who refused to fit the current feminine stereotype. Historically, their lifestyle violated standards of American manners and morals as dictated by the Protestant church in the last century. As late as the 1950s, when she left high school, an actress tells me, she remembers that part of the reason she chose to go to the Goodman School in Chicago was that she knew she was choosing a freer lifestyle.

Since many women outside theater now enjoy that option, other qualities in actresses may have become more apparent. A young actress in her first professional job talks about gathering her reserves of energy to "step into the aura" of the actors with whom she works. Other actresses recognize her experience and talk about the excitement of "playing to strength" and the exhilaration they feel in it. It is in this sense that the risk of confrontation and conflict and the control of energy expended seem to be special attractions to the women interviewed here. As more and more women chose acting because of lessening social pressures and increased educational opportunities, the competition between women increases and women begin to pursue their careers more aggressively in order to be able to work. However, a woman who becomes an actress must be capable of portraying the stereotypical loving, caring, "soft" woman, particularly in the commercial theater. For actresses, that image is still the bread and butter of the business especially in films and television.

It is equally clear that in their personal lives, women in the theater tend to rely on their own physical, emotional and psychological resources. An actress who has made her career in regional theater says

Just to work in the theater, you have to be capable of leasing your apartment, . . . of going to [another] city. You're capable of organizing yourself in a way that you can afford to do that.

Only once did I meet a woman who was totally helpless. She just never worked out of town. She had two teenage sons and her husband worked for CBS and she never left her home. She had no idea how to hire somebody to feed her family. This was a very consciousness-raising experience for her, to see how her family managed in her absence. Her guilt at leaving these people was very unusual. . . . This was at a time when I had a seven-year-old at home and a husband who worked full time. I had everything organized including notes about what they were going to defrost that night.

An older actress preparing herself for a heavy part in a long tour takes an unsentimental, no-nonsense attitude toward her self-sufficiency. She points out that touring is much more humane for actors today than it was a century ago.

My friend [an older British actress] was always saying, I hope someone is cosseting you. That word cosset! And I'd say, I have no one to cosset me except myself. Cosseting has something to do with the littlest lamb—you take care of the little lamb and nurture him and shield him. That sort of thing. Well, that's all very nice. But the actor nowadays, when you think of what the actor a hundred years ago had to go through, we have it very easy. Still and all, the work itself is demanding . . . you do have to be careful. Sometimes you go through periods of sleeplessness where you seem to get charged and then it's hard to relax and slow down. Then I have to take a massage or a long walk or sit in the sauna. Something like that.

As women are encouraged by less constricting societal attitudes and by the changing expectation that women need or may no longer depend upon a husband for economic support, perhaps it is not surprising that many of them are choosing a profession in which they can explore both their own personalities and the world they live in.

Status and Respectability in University Training

The burgeoning field of theater education has drastically changed the route into the profession of acting over the past 40 years. University training in which graduate school is emphasized has provided both the status of advanced education and a more protected environment for learning the craft. Before so many of these programs were instituted, actresses describe leaving high school or college in 1935 or 1950 to look for work in the New York theater and, within a short time, being cast in shows. An older actress's comments indicate how much easier it was to get work and how different the training was for a young ingenue in the star system of the 1930s.

> I feel so sorry for kids today. It's so different. I got three shows that first year. The first one was a tryout with a famous comedienne. She was married to the producer. I went on the road for three months while they tried to get the play right and they couldn't.
> So by the time I came back I had three months work with a very tough actress. I felt I was a professional by that time. If I had any bad habits, she got them out of me. . . . She was very demanding and very professional. And I had never been in a professional play before. If I moved on her line or did anything I wasn't supposed to do, she would take me offstage and give me a slap. I learned fast, I tell you.

Today universities all over the country maintain extensive professional theater training programs that often require six years of college. Many of these schools draw from the same theoretical base thus providing their graduates with a common vocabulary if not a common method of work. Many university programs have developed connections with theaters which provide opportunities to their students. Until recently, Arena Stage in Washington was headed by Zelda Fichandler who directs the graduate theater program at NYU. Yale Drama School maintains connections with Yale Repertory Theater which has begun to bring its productions of new playwrights into New York. Duke University offers its elaborate theatrical plant and its technical facilities to producers for pre–Broadway tryouts. Students who go through these programs have the opportunity to make contacts that will open doors for them as they begin their careers.

All of these changes in education have given both young men and women the opportunity to learn and perform in a more forgiving environment than they would encounter in the real theater. University theaters are often state-of-the-art facilities with computerized equipment and advanced technology. Young people can learn to use the kind of equipment that older or smaller theaters do not have or cannot afford.

Academic theater also offers additional lucrative jobs for trained theater professionals. A position with a college or university can be a source of dependable income for a period of several years and can actually provide the actor, writer or director with artistic breathing space between difficult or risky projects. Performers, stage managers, directors, administrators, and playwrights often move between teaching, developing graduate programs, artist-in-residence positions, and the working theater. For the young performer, the advantage of this link between academic and working theater is that it often becomes a support network for getting jobs.

The Regional Theater Movement and Women

The idea of a socially relevant theater in this country is usually associated with Jane Addams at Hull House in Chicago. Working with an immigrant community in the late 1800s, she recognized the group's attraction to the popular melodramas produced at local theaters. She began to see that "a theater which depicted life more truthfully would attract the young people of the neighborhood and would encourage understanding in place of escape" (Chinoy and Jenkins 1987, 199).

It was from this frame of reference, bringing theater classics and innovative new plays to a wider audience outside of the artistically conservative, commercial climate of New York, that regional theaters spread across the country in the 1950s. Through the vision and creative energies of producer-directors Margo Jones, Nina Vance, and Zelda Fichandler, these theaters provided artists with a more stable environment in which to perform Shakespeare, Molière, Chekhov, and Shaw as well as to experiment with new works. A standard of living and a quality of life was, and still is, available to performers in these areas that would be unaffordable in Manhattan. Marriages can be maintained and children can be nurtured. When I asked a young actress in New York if she ever thinks about the quality of life available elsewhere, she said, "all the time."

In establishing professional acting companies outside New York in cities across the country, regional theaters educated a theater-going audience to a certain standard of artistic achievement and production values. According to an Equity newsletter survey, these theaters, operating under the League of Regional Theaters (LORT) contract, generated more work for performers than did Broadway or touring companies in 1987. *New York Times* critic Frank Rich has observed that the New York stage regularly draws on the creative vitality of these theaters to produce new works. Many serious American playwrights have developed their craft at theaters outside of New York. Many performers have grown into extraordinary talents working at these theaters.

Derrick Lee Weeden, Laurie Birmingham, and Monica Bell in *Tartuffe* by Molière. Photographer: Scarsbrook. Courtesy of Alabama Shakespeare Festival.

What do regional theaters mean for women? Though the original impetus came from the creative energies of a number of remarkable women, regional theaters were never envisioned as feminist theaters. They have always functioned as mainstream theaters that employed talented men and women with no special frame of reference for gender. One could even argue that since a mainstay of their repertoire has frequently been older plays and classics, most of the performers they employ have been men.

In recent years, however, they have begun to nurture women playwrights. And in Washington, D.C., a sizable number of small theaters that function just below the level of LORT contract theaters do so under the leadership of women. So at certain levels of theater, there are a healthy number of women in management positions. Whether or not that has any effect on the status of women who are performers is unclear.

What can benefit the actress in this type of theater is the more adventurous casting and quality of the plays that are performed. New plays that focus on the lives of women in more substantive ways are more often produced and developed at regional theaters than in New York. While the rehearsal atmosphere especially for a new play

Sabrina Le Beauf as Rosalind in *As You Like It*. Photographer: Joan Marcus. Courtesy of Shakespeare Theatre at the Folger.

may be tense, the whole set of pressures that attend a New York opening (critics, money, reputations on the line) will not be over-whelming. Interesting failures can be rewarding experiences out of town.

Actresses who are raising children often find that they can make a satisfying career working in one geographic area. If they grow into leading ladies at these theaters, they may become extraordinary ac-tresses with the ability to play Shakespeare, Brecht, Kaufman and Hart, or Sam Shepard. They eventually acquire a résumé of work ex-perience that is enormous by today's standards.

However, mobility is still an important factor for performers in a competitive job market and women who chose to work only in one place necessarily limit their careers. Regional theater offers the op-portunity to work on plays that examine the lives of women in deeper ways and to explore aspects of life, kinds of people, and sub-ject matter once thought of as unsuitable for the stage. When per-formers talk optimistically about plays by and about women, they often mention, *'night Mother* and *Crimes of the Heart*. There is a strain of black humor in both these works that stands in sharp con-trast to earlier, more sentimentalized characterizations of women. That audiences find these plays compelling encourages the explora-tion of other difficult areas of women's lives. Actresses have better

Ruby Dee, Tonia Rowe, and Jonathan Earl Peck in *The Glass Menagerie* by Arthur Miller. Photographer: Joan Marcus. Courtesy of Arena Stage.

opportunities in such plays to use their life experience to fully humanize complex characters in such a way that they and the audience recognize real people.

Nontraditional Casting

More adventurous casting choices by directors and administrators is still a problem in New York and elsewhere. In the early 1980s in Washington, a Black actress gave up her place in an established company because in two years she had played nothing but walk- ons and maids. A white actress who was shocked at that situation feels that theater has an obligation to turn over older stereotypes and enlarge the vision of the audience.

> She could have played many roles. . . . An audience isn't going to accept it until it's done. But that's why it needs to be done: so that it's not an issue. You just have to do it boldly, and they're so tentative, the administration, not trusting that the audience will accept it. I think as long as you want to please the audience, if you did everything to make it easy for them, plays would be boring.

During the same period, another Equity company in D.C. began to feature one Black actress in such roles as Lady Macbeth, Cleopatra, and Paulina in *Winter's Tale*. Another played Rosalind in *As You Like It*. In 1986, the League of Washington Theaters established a council of representatives who would explore specific ways for theaters to open up more roles to minority performers and women. Since then, Washington has seen Black productions of *Glass Menagerie*, a Trinidadian adaptation of *Playboy of the Western World* and a number of new works by Black playwrights. Generally, there has been more integrated casting of minority performers in bigger roles at Equity theaters. An Asian-American Miranda in *The Tempest* comes to mind as a casting choice that worked particularly well for the play.

In New York, plays by August Wilson have been brought into town through the efforts of Yale Repertory and a collaboration of producers including the Center Theatre Group, the Ahmanson, Huntington Theatre Center, the O'Neill Center, the Goodman Theatre, and the Old Globe. In a recent PBS interview, a Black director remembers that he had the same difficulty finding Broadway producers for Lorraine Hansberry's *Raisin in the Sun* 30 years previously as he had for Wilson's *Piano Lesson*.

Two stories from Black actresses, one in New York and one outside the city, illustrate how tentative directors and theater management can be on the subject of color. I went to see a friend in an Off Broadway production and was impressed with what appeared to be a nontraditional casting choice. When I spoke to the Black actress who played the role afterwards, she laughed and told me a less encouraging story.

> I was a reader for the auditions for [the director] and at the end of the day, I said, may I audition for you now. He said, sure but I don't really need to see you. Your reading's been wonderful. He basically knew what I could do. I auditioned for him [previously] for *The Marriage of Bette and Boo* and he informed me that I was Black. I said I knew that. He [told] me that because of the nature of *Bette and Boo* which was an Irish Catholic nuclear family, he couldn't see his way to casting a Black person. The play didn't deal with that. And I understood.
>
> Then [this play] came along. Again, I understood intellectually. Of course, it hurt me. I understood what he was saying, that this play was written for a company and the situation in that company at that time was that they had no Black members and they wanted to address the question of race. So they solved the problem by casting [a white actor] as the Black man. That was the comment for the original production.
>
> So for this particular production, the director had problems with a Black being in the play because in a way the problem had already been solved and it would seem like an artistic non sequitur, an additional comment, that he wasn't sure he was willing to make.
>
> Then the lady who was originally cast dropped out, got a very good gig elsewhere, and I was put into the play. About three days later, the director commented to me that it made no difference because everybody treated me as what the character was, not as a Black and that was the bottom line. That's how I got in the show. I hope he learned that lesson, damn it.

The second story comes from an actress who took a job with a stock theater in Pennsylvania. They had decided that "breaking the color barrier" was something that they wanted to do. In her mid-twenties and from Jersey City, the actress had never heard herself described as part of a "colored couple" before.

> I was a total fool when I took that summer stock thing. We were the first Blacks on [that] stage. I think that's what caught on, and they

kept us. I thought it was weird because they kept saying to me the first week, so how do you like it? And they were talking about the people in the town. I didn't even get it because if you're not used to that, [you don't notice it]. I would just drift around. People were looking at me funny but people look funny anyway so I just thought it was what I was wearing. I didn't get it. Black families began to stop me and say, do you know where you are? That's when I got it.

But they [the management] were really afraid. . . . People would write in and say "we were so happy to see a 'colored couple' on stage." Colored couple! "And you keep using them as you see necessary."

For Black actresses, as for other minority performers, nontraditional casting can mean the difference between being able to explore the full range of human experience or being confined to someone else's limited view of being Black. Several young actresses say there are no roles for them. One asks, "why aren't there plays that deal with now, with today's women? *Raisin's* fine but that's dated. No one's talking about what's going on now. . . . [N]o one's talking about something we don't already know. That's where men have it better."

Another actress who is a veteran of radio, television, film and stage work speaks to the entrenched idea that minority performers can play only certain limited roles that have commercial value or credibility even for the minority audience.

[In regard to] What's acceptable for Black actors, there's such a limited thinking in the minds of critics particularly. They've teethed on stereotypes and old notions, . . . the public is [more accepting]. . . . But those people who put money in things are much less daring.

She has spent half a lifetime assuring whoever would listen that there is a sizable body of Black history that chronicles a far more varied culture than the exotic underworld that is usually thought to hold the interest of general audiences.

At this age now I don't feel like dealing with the ignorance. I don't feel like going through the history of the Black middle class. The cotillions. The coming-out parties. My uncle was considered a millionaire in the thirties. Landowners. Also slave owners, too, who were Black. So I find myself impatient. I want somebody else to instruct, or say, here's a little card with all these books. Go read these books. All these years . . . you're answering the same kindergarten questions.

Talking about the rich resource of Black novels that she is still trying to promote as television or film projects, she says, "I hope I

Pat Carroll as Sir John Falstaff. Photographer: Joan Marcus. Courtesy of Shakespeare Theatre at the Folger.

shan't be too old by the time I get them realized. . . . these are the writers I've wanted to do for so many years and nothing's happened. . . . Somebody says they're going to do them. They don't do them. Years go by and nothing gets done."

Although nontraditional casting has had increased relative success in some areas, the comments of an actor-director indicate that the concept may seem equitable but is not an easy one to use in a small company. His experience is probably not an isolated one.

> I was . . . accused of casting bias by putting a male into a female part . . . the decision came down between a man and a woman and I choose the male actor for balance and talent. The actress had a very rough time accepting this decision but I truly feel it was made from a theatrical view as opposed to a gender issue. In the same show, I offered a male part to a woman but she declined.

Competition appears to be so strong among younger groups of performers that when nontraditional casting means gender-switching, additional competition between men and women adds more strain to working relationships. There is a long-standing tradition in the theater that certain older women's roles may be played by men. Older actresses remark on how the practice of gender-switching works against them. With only so many good roles to look forward to, it is hard to see Lady Bracknell and Mistress Quickly go to a man. Two recent Shakespeare productions in D.C. in which Falstaff and Puck were played by actresses indicate that innovative casting can make this tradition work both ways. An actress concedes this but says, "we win some, but not as many."

Age Bias Against Women

Sitting across the table from an actress who I know is the same age as myself, I look for lines in her face and see none. Watching her work on stage, I see her only as the age of the part she is playing. Youth and age are often accomplished on the stage through behavior. In the same theater season, I have seen an actor in his late twenties play a nine-year-old and an older actress embody first the incontinence of old age and then the winsomeness of youth in one role.

Another actress without a line in her face remembers sitting down to the make-up mirror and discovering the ravages of long hours at two jobs staring back at her. Every performance begins in front of the mirror. Every performer makes the best of what he or she chooses to see there. In this sense, time and the natural aging process is the enemy of everyone in the theater with the possible exception of 29-year-old character men. Still, in the theater the preoccupation with youth that is generally apparent in American society works against women more heavily than men. "Our society is ageist," says an actor, who points to the lack of concern for older people in general, an entertainment and music industry focused on the 18 to 35 age group, and the specific problems of women.

In thinking about the different experience that actors and actresses have in getting jobs as they grow older, the following contrast comes to mind. A character actor who had enjoyed his career in regional theater for most of his life had a sudden burst of film roles in his mid-sixties. He told a friend that he had begun to feel that the great thing for an actor was longevity. He said, "I'm sixty-six. I'm not a great actor, but I'm little and I'm cute and I'm still here. And now everybody wants to hire me."

Auditioning is quite a different experience for an actress in her fifties who did her first Broadway show when she was 17. She often goes to audition for parts in her age range and is told she is too chic-looking. Her agent suggests that she keep some old clothes to wear to these readings but she feels that this is insulting to her profession and to her own self-respect. She says, "I don't mind if they see me the way I look normally and they say, would you mind changing? I will do that … but I don't want to go in looking like some poor downtrodden actress who never works or like I need a meal."

The point she makes is well taken. All performers dress carefully in going for jobs and no older actor would allow himself to look shabby for a reading. She also suggests that women in their middle years do not look the way they did a generation ago. Better health care, an emphasis on diet and exercise, and changes in lifestyle generally have made it difficult to tell the difference between 45 and 55. Since this is the age group where there is money and time to go to the theater, it seems unfortunate that the stereotype largely precludes the existence of youthful-looking mature women.

> I don't think it's right that people have to lie about their age and yet if you don't, people say, oh God, can she learn her lines, does she have arthritis. The average conception of an older actress today [55 to 65] is that she should be portly or a skinny bent-over woman with grey hair. But we don't look like that. Women today aren't like they were twenty-five years ago. We're different from people a generation ago and that has to be recognized. There have to be a whole lot of people out there who are over fifty years old. There shouldn't be a stereotype.

This is not to say that actors who have established careers playing leading men do not have difficulty when they must make the transition to playing older character roles in order to continue working. Some of these men make that transition quite late. A young actor asks me why it is that women viewers apparently continue to find older actors romantically interesting on shows like "Dynasty" and "Falcon Crest." My answer is that I don't know that they do.

It's been my experience that casting decisions are not made on the basis of fan mail but on what producers consider to be the drawing power of a star. An actress over 50 who has had a long career on stage and in films and television extends this thought in the following comments, but feels that the stage is more forgiving to age than are movies and television.

> Women are not permitted to get older and still be desirable. Men
> definitely are. Gary Cooper got to play the love interest with
> Audrey Hepburn. . . . Bette Davis and Joan Crawford had to do hor-
> ror films. But the theater is more liberal than other fields. Movies
> are second and TV is still the least liberal regarding age and gender.
> It's the popular medium.

When actors find they must move from one generation of roles
to the next, there are interesting, well-written roles to which they
can go. Not only are there fewer parts for women but heavier
stereotyping means that the range and continuum of roles are more
limited than those available to men. An actress who is also a director
says

> Women don't seem to be thought of as doers and molders of events
> in society. Consequently, once our romantic, marrying, childbearing
> years are over, we are in a sense put out to pasture.

She also adds that although this bias in the way women are
represented is problematic for actresses, she herself has never felt
particularly discriminated against as an artist. The theater is a
naturally "discriminatory profession" in the sense that jobs are not
easy to get for any group. Fairness has never been a factor in the
audition process. But the most cogent argument for using some
degree of affirmative action on behalf of women and minorities including older performers would seem to be that the real world has
changed and if the theater proposes to show us that world, it should
change as well.

What About Those Women in Shakespeare?

In looking at the number of parts for women in the older
literature of the theater, Shakespeare becomes an interesting test
case. For both women and men who perform his plays, there is a particularly personal bond that forms between the player and the playwright. A young actor working in his first Shakespeare describes his
feeling that the man himself is standing at the edge of the stage watching a scene, muttering encouragement. Frustrated that she cannot
time her stage business so that it gives emphasis to a long speech, an
actress says, "Oh Will, let's cut it." Performers never have any doubt
that one man, whoever he was, wrote the plays. They can feel one

Harriet Harris as Titania, Lynn Chausow as Puck, and Peter Francis-James as Oberon in *Midsummer Night's Dream.* **Photographer: Joe Giannetti. Courtesy of the Guthrie Theater.**

mind developing a particular set of ideas from one play to the next as they do them. They also feel that he was someone who lived and worked in the theater as they do. He leans on the stage and speaks to them from 400 years ago. They recognize him as one of them.

Since this is the classical playwright who enjoys unqualified affection, it is interesting to see what performers think of the representation of women in his plays. I was surprised to hear from a number of actors who have spent a good part of their careers performing Shakespeare that the parts were not written for women and it is a tribute to the playwright that women can play them. Although it is historically true that in the Elizabethan theater, women's roles were played by boys, that fact has never occurred to me while I was watching a performance of the plays. Whoever Shakespeare had in mind when he wrote them, the modern audience recognizes the female characters in his plays as women. Indeed Virginia Woolf points out in her long essay on women writers, that when one considers the small number of written accounts either by or about women from that period, the women in Shakespeare's plays take on an added significance as eyewitness accounts of either people he knew or at least the cultural norm for women in England at that time (Woolf 1929).

In his one-man performance of scenes from Shakespeare, Ian McKellen finishes a speech of Juliet's and asks the audience how a teenage boy could be trained to feel and express this range of emotion. He himself has just given a good example of it.

An actress points out another archaic tradition in post–Elizabethan theater that took a different view of the mature actress than the one currently in vogue.

> In the old Shakespearean theater, a woman didn't play Juliet until she was thirty-five because [it was thought] she wasn't capable of understanding that kind of love until she was that old. But it's not like that anymore. . . . Hollywood doesn't hesitate for a minute to cast a fifty-year-old man in a younger role but they wouldn't do it for a woman.

An actress who played Juliet at the beginning of her career and found it difficult points out one of the qualities that performers value in the plays: the carefully-crafted, special voice of even the smallest characters. She makes an argument that draws on what is known of Shakespeare's personal history.

> It's like a painter. If a painter painted Juliet, he wouldn't paint her as a man. And Shakespeare, even though he knew a boy would play the part, it was still the portrait of a woman.
>
> It's interesting when you read about the history of when he wrote the particular plays. *King John* came after his son died. Constance (who thinks her son is dead) just pours out this scene of grief that's absolutely searing. So it's interesting that he wrote that then.
>
> And also Lear for Cordelia, that grief is so personal, so absolutely specific that you know he was in touch with all kinds of human feel-

ings and had gone through many of them. He was a master at making them very specific. I always think of that line of Juliet's, when she says "the more I give to thee, the more I have, for both are infinite." In the act of giving love, you get it back. He knew that.

Shakespeare was swell, one of those geniuses of the world who knew it all. But I think he was a very great artist in that he gave specific voices to both men and women and you couldn't possibly mix them up.

Some performers see no gender specificity at all in the plays. "Shakespeare is about ideas and verse. I can see Hamlet being done by a woman." Indeed, in the 19th century a number of American actresses made their reputations doing the male roles in Shakespeare.

A British actress talks about the range of opportunities for developing one's technique and stretching artistically for both men and women in the classics.

What I have to do is a forty-line speech, which contains only...
domestic sentiment, but uses rich imagery, poetic devices, humour, different tactics, energy focused first here and then there. The story's the same [as a film script or television play], but the requirements of technique and physical range and stamina are so much bigger. That's why I went to the RSC because Shakespeare gives you the opportunity to use your stagecraft, and that's something that's equal across the board. It's as difficult for a man to say that verse as it is for a woman. There's as much mind and heart to link up, as much technique and emotion – all those challenges set by the verse [Todd 1984, 17].

In looking at this one small area of gender relationships, in various performers' perspectives on the women in Shakespeare, it is possible to see the initial difficulty that women face in theater. There are more parts written for men and those parts are larger and more pivotal to the action of the play.

However, Shakespeare gave very specific voices to the female characters in his plays. Stereotypes are difficult to find. The multiple responsibilities with which women have always struggled are represented in a broad range of ages and stations in life. Maturity and age retain the vigor of their sexuality. The requirements of the language set a challenge that is as difficult to accomplish for men as it is for women.

Since the early days of theater in this country, Black performers have found expression for their talent in Shakespeare. Perhaps 400 years of historical distance permits acceptance of this. There are two ways to approach meaning in classical works. One is to preserve the period, the style, and the original context of the play. The other is to adapt those elements and examine what the play has to say to a modern audience. Casting minority performers in critical roles has accomplished this particularly well. Minority performers have found challenging roles and full expression for their humanity in Shakespeare when they could not always find it elsewhere.

Likewise actresses who study Shakespeare's women to play them find a recognizable expression of their own human experience and for that reason, there will probably always be "someone who's willing to play the maid." The part may be small but it's there and it's not underwritten.

TWO

LOWER PAY, LESS VOICE
HURT THE STATUS
OF WOMEN

Eleanor Leacock is one of a number of anthropologists who are unwilling to generalize about the secondary status of women. She points out that women everywhere make a substantial economic contribution to society. Her work links the status of women to access to resources, the conditions of their work and the material reimbursement for labor (Moore 1988).

Other anthropologists who work in gender studies have indicated a connection between the value of the laborer and the value of his or her labor, and the influence of this estimate of worth on concepts of self, personhood, and autonomy (Moore 1988). It is in reference to these relationships that it is useful to look at how the working lives of actresses are affected by some attitudes associated with salary differences and sexual harassment.

Both inequalities in pay and the opportunism sometimes directed at women in the work place can be related to the basic fact that there are too many actresses competing for too few jobs. But this general statement does not elucidate the specifically damaging effects of salary differences and working conditions on the performer. Acting is a profession where self-confidence and personal assurance are crucial. In auditions, readings, and meetings with casting people and agents, performers – like salespeople – are marketing not only their talent, training, and experience. They are also trying to project a particular set of physical characteristics and a personality that is at ease with itself in front of strangers. This is difficult enough to do given the current levels of competition in the profession. Any circumstance that diminishes self-esteem or sense of personal worth makes the process even harder. The actress needs an extra measure of confidence in herself if she has had experience in contract negotiations or the work environment that devalues the essential nature of her gender.

An additional problem exists if sexual harassment impacts on the creative process. Women who feel that they have somehow failed to effectively resolve repeated incidents may find that they develop a block in their work which limits artistic growth. For these reasons, these two difficult subjects are worth examination.

Women Work Cheap

So many interpretations of status militate against asking how much money a performer is making in a particular job. There are innumerable ways of compensating actors and these grow even more complex in film and television contracts. As the wife of an actor, I have often been the focus of a negotiated transportation item in contracts, an airplane ticket for the wife. Since union contracts dictate that performers must be provided with first class transportation in certain circumstances, whether or not the wife goes first class as well can become another negotiating point. I would guess that husbands of actresses have had the same experience.

Union salaries set a basic minimum for everyone which varies as it applies to the type of theater contract, Broadway, LORT (League of Regional Theaters), dinner theater, or other. Above the minimum, salaries are negotiated through agents or by individual performers. "Favored nation" riders to contracts add another level of arcane stipulations in which salary, transportation, housing, dressing rooms, per diem, or billing are negotiated at the same level as other performers in the cast. "Favored nation" riders can serve to simplify contract negotiations or they can be used by agents, performers, or producers to manipulate those terms in various ways for profit, protection, or status. Performers are generally suspicious of the "favored nations" contract in which all salaries are equal. Those with heavy roles are often asked to take less than their usual quote and those in smaller roles never believe that everybody is getting the same money.

Nonunion theaters may pay a set fee, or cut-of-the-house, or nothing at all.

In 1986, Equity instituted a new contract that allows Equity members to work at small nonunion theaters for less than union minimum. This contract appears to benefit performers in their twenties because they can work more often in larger roles where they learn to carry the burden of the play. But they cannot do this for any long period of time because they are not being paid a living wage. For Equity members who had already begun to work at small theaters under the older letter of agreement contract, the new arrangement means that theaters can legally pay them much less. One reason for allowing the small theater contract, according to the union, is that many Equity members felt they needed these theaters in order to develop their skills and showcase their work. This argument assumes that if these small theaters are given the time to grow, eventually they may become union houses that would then pay full Equity salaries.

Are women generally paid less than men for stage work? A woman who has been an agent in New York for 15 years does not think so. In contrast, the male half of an acting couple says that he assumes that actresses are paid less than actors. He has worked at several theaters with his wife. An actress remembers her anger when she discovered that an actor with a tiny part in the show where she was playing the lead was making the same salary that she had to bargain for vigorously. My information on theater salaries for men and women is anecdotal but the situation of greater competition for fewer roles suggests a disadvantage in the bargaining position for women.

If what establishes the value of a resource is its scarcity, actresses are in over-supply. Even though Equity figures for 1988 show membership at 47 percent female and 53 percent male, the numbers of women auditioning for the same part strikes many in the profession as remarkable. An actor remembers that while dropping off his wife's résumé at a television producer's office he was stunned to see that the line of actresses waiting to audition for a supporting role in a new series extended out of the building and around the corner. This high level of competition requires women to regularly summon special resources of confidence, both in themselves and their work.

From where does this confidence come in a profession offering limited opportunities, intense competition, lack of job security, and

frequent opportunities for rejection? Based on the kinds of
strategies that actresses use to find solutions to their problems, I
think some measure of personal confidence comes out of the experience of performance.

The point of the next long description is not that an actress was
paid less but that she weighed the risks and took the job instead of
backing away from an inherently confrontational situation. If risk
and control are elements of dramatic conflict that become familiar
devices to performers in the professional situation, might they not
also be familiar devices that performers feel equipped to deal with
in personal situations as well? I do not mean to suggest that performers readily manipulate personal situations to their advantage.
My point is that the actress in question acted without fear of conflict.
She was angry but she proceeded with assurance and she was not
intimidated.

When I first interviewed the actress who told me the following
story, she said that she had never felt any kind of discrimination in
her work. Some months later the following experience made her a
strong advocate for equitable treatment of women in theater and in
society. In what may be a worst case scenario, the producer of a
regional Shakespeare festival was a shock to both the actress and
her agent in his attitude toward women. It is no great revelation to
say that women are paid less than men in many professions besides
acting, but it is still surprising to have a potential employer state this
as a matter of policy in contract negotiations.

The actress began her story by saying that the producer in question is from Taiwan "so he does carry all that Old World stuff with
him."

A director friend who was planning a production of *Hamlet* at
the festival in question came to see her in a production where she had
made some bold choices, and offered her the part of Gertrude.

I sent my picture and résumé to the festival and I was offered
Tamara in *Titus Andronicus* as well. I was initially quoted $550 a
week for doing the two roles which I thought was respectable. I was
assured that that was what all the guest artists were making (four
actors, one actress). I was the first female guest artist ever in the
history of the festival [which] is about fifteen to twenty years old.
Before that, they used a lot of students [for the women's roles].

So I was initially quoted $550 a week. That was before I had ac-
cepted the job. I had just gotten this new agent. I said to them, yes,
I'd be glad to do those roles but you need to talk to my agent. I need

this to go through him. When the agent negotiated with [the producer], the producer brought it down to $325 a week for doing Gertrude in *Hamlet* and Tamara in *Titus*, and Tamara is the female lead.

When my agent said we were quoted $550, the producer went off the wall and said to my agent, "women work cheap! I can get women cheap! I don't know why this actress thinks she should get $550." My agent had found out the men in the company were getting $500 but when he asked about it, the producer said, "that's because the men are teaching as well." As it turned out, only one of them was teaching and yet they were all getting $500.

So my agent said, "Well, $325 is unacceptable. Let's face it, you have an actress who is capable of doing those two parts and you're not going to find a young non–Equity actress who can carry both roles," and he talked him up to $400. I said my bottom line was $450 but they got up to $400 and then it was nonnegotiable. So I took it. My agent was very distressed at me taking it but I wanted to do the roles and I knew I wouldn't have another opportunity to do Gertrude for quite a long time – I'm thirty-three. Also I wanted to work with [the actor playing Hamlet] and I wanted to do Tamara because how often do you get to do *Titus*. So I figured it was a good swap. But I went out there knowing the guy was a misogynist, knowing what he had said. So I knew there would be some problems.

In the second half of her story, what is surprising is how badly the producer had underestimated the actress he had hired. The "administration" of the theater in requesting the Equity performers to elect a deputy, should have been more familiar with the duties of that position or more concerned with who was elected. The job of Equity deputy is often one that no one in a company wants. It makes extra demands on time and energy and risks confrontation with management. The actress was elected. Not only did she take the job seriously, but she knew both the specific terms of the guest artist contract and the Equity rule book. The situation suggests that although this producer had been running the theater for some years, this was his first experience with someone who took appropriate union action against him.

I ended up being the deputy. Normally, there aren't deputies for guest artists but there were five of us and we needed some kind of protection. The nonunion people had a deputy of their own. They had built that into the structure of the administration and they had requested that the union people have a deputy. So I ended up being the deputy. It was ironic that they'd never had one before and now here I was the deputy.

The guest artist contract was very specific about overtime. They were allowed a seven-hour day. For anything over that, they had to pay X amount–I think it was ten or fifteen every half hour. Then if they violated the twelve-hour period of rest, that was another twenty-five or something like that. Well, they were really breaking contract left, right, and center with the overtime infractions. Rehearsal schedules were not well thought out. They were pushing their limits and it didn't look like they were going to pay. So I brought it up when I was invited to a production meeting.

I was asked to talk about how the actors were feeling about things. And I said, "As far as the union people are concerned, contract is being broken, and it doesn't appear that you're willing to pay. As deputy, you have to know that it's my job to report this to the union." The producer was there and he flew off the handle and said, "You union people are lucky to have this job!" He put it in the feminine. He said, "In years past, actresses would come here and work for us under an assumed name so that they could take the job. You're lucky to be working!" I just let that go and I said, "Be that as it may, contract is being broken. You need to pay overtime. I shouldn't be having this conversation with you face to face. It should be between you and the union."

So I called the union in LA and explained and they took it from there. But I got a very angry letter from the producer saying, you bad little girl, how dare you call the union. For him, it was an enormous loss of face. He had this big parental Daddy thing that I had misbehaved. It was a horrible letter.

I marched over to his office with the letter in hand and explained to him in a very loud voice that it's the deputy's job to record overtime and if I hadn't reported it, I wouldn't have been doing my job. I explained the procedure to him, the time sheets a deputy fills out, all of that. He got very small and then did apologize.

What made it worse was that there was an actor in *Titus* who would go to the office once a week to complain about union infractions, and it was always taken care of. But when I went through the union, I got this nasty letter. The overtime turned out to be an extra $100 an actor. I burned the letter, it made me so angry. I called the union and talked to them about it. They wished I had saved it because they were ready to press harassment charges. I had never experienced sexism before but this was blatant. To have him say, women work cheap, was a real slap in the face.

It is possible to look at the resolution of this incident as a model of how the protections set in place by the union (the deputy, the time sheets, and union arbitration) are supposed to work for the performer. However, the model depends for its effectiveness on the deputy's knowledge of the contract and union procedure. The deputy must also have the fortitude to insist that those obligations be met.

When this must be done in a public situation, such as a production meeting or a rehearsal, many performers are reluctant to appear uncooperative with directors or producers, and thus endangering future employment.

Probably an important factor in this situation is that the actress accepted the job as a one-time opportunity to do roles that she knew would add to her experience. She accepted less money than was originally offered because she thought it was "a good swap." Most performers would agree with her that good roles are a convincing argument for taking a job for less money. As she was aware of the producer's attitude toward women, she had no expectation of continuing to work at that theater. She accepted the position of Equity deputy when she could have avoided it on the grounds that any of the actors might be a more influential negotiator than a woman. She was confident enough in her artistic work that the producer would not be able to find an excuse to convince the director to terminate her contract. So it did not occur to her to try to protect her job in any way. She expected the theater to honor all contractual obligations and assumed that the union would support that expectation. Her straightforward attitude may have been influenced by standards set at theaters where she had previously worked.

Her anger at the producer's estimate of the value of women may be partly an effect of her age (she tells us she is 33). Processes of socialization have fortified a younger generation of women with a more demanding set of expectations than women previously had. For whatever reasons, her direct approach and confidence in the justification of her actions brought an effective resolution to what could have been a bad work situation.

Her own explanation of her actions is that she associates the response she made with the level of work she was doing at that time. It was part of what she found in the exploration that she was doing for a number of productions. "It was a real lesson to me on sexism and my stand on it. Up to this summer, I didn't really know where I stood. I didn't have any real anger myself . . . [then] it suddenly became this big political issue with me as well as a personal issue. I think it coincided with my work, coming to find what my own voice is."

The producer in question undoubtedly still believes that women work cheap, but he also knows that there are women who will challenge his attitude and that they are supported by effective organizational tools that they know how to use in their defense.

Most People Will Say It's Not That Big a Deal But It **Is** That Big a Deal!

"It really depresses me. There's a lot of sexism in America." These comments come from an actress/playwright who lives and works in Manhattan. She is a pretty woman with the courage to do theater in prisons in the New York area. "Most people will say when it comes right down to it, it really isn't that big a deal. But it really *is* that big a deal. It diminishes how you think about your own sex."

Actresses rarely talk about threatening instances of sexual harassment. It's possible that they do not want to encourage outsiders to believe that this is a profession where "these things happen." One of the reasons sometimes given for choosing to ignore harassment is the temporary nature of the work. It may be easier to put up with a difficult situation if it is only going to last for a few days or a few weeks. This is a strategy for dealing with unpleasant experiences by ignoring and making a definite effort to forget them. Self-esteem, however, is not bolstered by calling up the details to recite to friends or interviewers.

There are opportunities for actresses to experience inappropriate behavior that confuses personal with professional life in auditions, the rehearsal environment, and performance. In audition situations, the actress can be made to feel that getting the job depends on her unqualified acceptance of whatever the director demands. This can apply to sexual behavior or nudity which may or may not be called for in the script.

An actress auditioning for a role in a Kennedy Center production had the following experience.

> Ninety percent of the piece I loved but for reasons that I never got any clear reading on. . .the goddess who runs through the piece is talking through a microphone at the beginning of the play and suddenly she starts rubbing the microphone on herself, having this sexual interaction with the microphone while she's talking. When I read it in the piece I said, "I don't understand why that is." When I saw it, I understood even less why she had to do that. The only justification I could see was that in his mind [the director's] the microphone was a phallic symbol and this woman could not hold it without having some sexual interaction with it. It had nothing to do with the play.

The same actress explains why it is important to her not to do work which seems to her to be exploitive.

As you mature in age and awareness, then your ability to ply your trade gets limited. ... There's less and less material that deals effectively with what's happening with you. Personally, artistically, philosophically, you're being offered things that are ... insulting to your intelligence [and] insulting to your life style ... maybe when you're twenty-two or twenty-five, you're excited about being an actor and you'll do just about anything. But as you get older, your consciousness deepens and you want to have the same integrity that you're experiencing in your life to be reflected in your work. When that is not there, I'd rather be a checker in the Safeway than to go on stage and do something I don't believe in.

I'm sure that is reflected to some degree in other professions but in the theater it's particularly acute because it's you up there and people question you and judge you based on what you do. So if you do something that is silly or degrading or less than you, you have to live with that. The process of being reviewed and scrutinized requires that you have to be some kind of strong person to not allow the comments that exist around actors and actresses to go in and make statements about you as a person. You really have to shore yourself up with some kind of steel wall to keep that from getting through and making a statement to you yourself about your own worthiness. So you begin to pick and chose your work very very carefully.

Union rules require that performers must be informed that nudity is required in the play before they take the part. But the way in which a director informs an actress can indicate to her that if she hesitates, her chances of getting the part are already diminished. A young actress had the following experience.

I did both my monologues, and he said, "That was fine but there's some nudity involved in this." I said, "I don't know if I could agree to it. I'd have to read the script and see if there's a point to it." When he saw that I was uncomfortable with it – and I was telling the truth, I did not say I'd do it because it was a job – he said, "Well, you know, most women would sign a contract right now." I said, "I don't know if I believe that."

I felt that because I wasn't willing to agree to it right away, somehow my sexuality was in question. I was a prude. But that's my right I think. ... He was saying that because I was uncomfortable with it, I was less of an actress. ... I don't believe that. ... That's just like being hit onstage. There are certain things that you have to live with for the rest of your life and that's one of them.

An actress explains the particularly vulnerable atmosphere that of necessity prevails during rehearsals. There are accepted standards of courtesy but they are not the same as one would find in other work environments. They can be easily imposed upon by directors or performers who choose to ignore them.

> The rules are so different. Your whole self is out. There are no rules of courtesy, the normal thing, and it's very hard to keep ... being totally open in rehearsal and in character, and then in informal offstage relationships you try and keep that limit but often it gets muddled. So you tend to be more open with the people you work with than you normally would be.
>
> In acting, your sexual energy and your performance energy and the interface between them is almost the same source. So it can be very volatile. ... It's an obvious trap [for both men and women] to let that be the source of their energy, the source of their part. When I was younger, I knew where I was getting that intensity and I let it happen but it confused me. Mentally, I didn't understand why it was working. Why was the attraction with this director, why is this the source of this role? I would accept it if it helped the role but it always bothered me. I felt this is not really the way ... to find the inner processes to understand the energy I want to draw on. You can get quite short-circuited with men. Where it has happened, it's always been a mutually understood thing ... [but] my energies were being used without me knowing what was happening.
>
> Often people I'm playing with are people I would have as my friends but [I wouldn't choose] to have a deeper relationship with them. And yet the deeper part of myself is what I want to open up and use onstage. The offstage stuff is often more troublesome for me. With a friend I can move from one thing to another and we respect the various shuttings-off. There's an instrument of understanding there. I'd like to have the [right] to choose and the space to be private.

Perhaps the most frightening kind of harassment that women experience comes from secretive behavior that can be hidden or excused by the forced intimacy of rehearsal or performance situations. Often the woman is not sure of what is happening until the behavior escalates and she feels she can neither avoid it nor stop it.

The example I have recorded comes from someone who was frightened by an episode of sexual harassment in her teen years when she was working in a theater company. Years later, she was still feeling its effects in personal strategies that she found she had unconsciously adopted to avoid another such episode and in the growing realization that she was becoming more and more distanced from the source of creative energies that she needed to be using in her work.

The farther you get away from yourself, the more terrifying it becomes. I could not do anything onstage or in an audition that was aggressive sexually. That had all been cut off for me. I was such a precocious kid and I equated being precocious with being handled that way. So I tried to be small and hidden and that's not my nature. I couldn't act. I couldn't feel anything. I couldn't cry.

This had begun to be a difficult situation for her in a profession where all thoughts and feelings must be available to be explored. As she says, "You've got to have an unobstructed path to your source of energy, whatever is down there that allows you to feel. . . . I felt like there was more and more in me as an actress that was dead space. I'd pick up a script and if it was something that made me uncomfortable, I would say it's a bad script." She was working on this problem with a therapist and in acting classes when the following incident occurred.

I thought, oh, God, I've got to prove to myself that I can deal with this. I probably over-dealt with it. I probably made him feel like a slug.

My size and my voice makes me appear to be younger than I am and that will sometimes be a problem. I said to my Mom, it's like I'm a magnet . . . for the kind of man who likes to see little girls from Catholic schools. I think he's gay but I also think he's many things and this is one of them. He grabbed my bottom a couple of times and I didn't like it and it scared me. That was early in rehearsal and then one night he sort of looked up and tried to put his head under it. I pushed him away but it was really shaking me up. I'd go home and call [her husband who was working out of town] and I was just terrified. It was hard to have him out of town but finally it was good that I had to deal with it myself. Now I feel I can always deal with it.

One night, he grabbed my bottom again and I just blew up. I said, "I hate it when that happens! Don't you ever do that again!" He said, "Oh, I guess I was being presumptuous." I said, "You have no right to touch my body."

Then we got into curtain calls and I had to hold his hand and he began to squeeze it really lightly, so disgusting, the kind of pause where he could always say, I didn't do anything. But there was something so like a mortician, so gross. He would give my hand this series of little pressures . . . it doesn't sound like much and yet, he was ignoring [the fact] that I had already told him that I hated this and he was nuts to bother me. Then he would not let go of my hand at the end of the curtain call.

I was terrified. It was bringing back a lot of bad memories, and I had a vague feeling of incompetence in that area. So I didn't speak to him for a month. . . . But the thing that I did was that I told everyone in the cast what was happening to me and that was the big difference, because, I thought, this is public knowledge now. Whether he knows it or not, everybody knows, and I didn't feel so alone. I've talked to other women about this and for some reason, sexual harassment makes you feel terribly alone. That doesn't happen to men. They don't realize that.

I told them, I've been through this before as a kid and I can't deal with it. So everybody watched out for me. He'd come near me and the women would close around me.

But then he cornered me one day and said, "I feel terrible about this. Can't we just be friends?" I said, "You should feel terrible about it. It's a repulsive way to treat another person." He said, "Well, I do. I feel very bad. I've just been hating myself." I said, "Don't hate yourself but don't look for total friendship either."

It is a deep unease that women have that men do not have. There is a type of man that is so tricky and that's where the violence is. I think that's what's so bone-chilling. You do end up feeling terribly trapped.

There were some guys in the cast who said, "Yeah, what's the big deal?" Another actor came to me and said, "This man is really upset about getting the chilly treatment. If you could be nice to him. He feels really bad and he understands he [shouldn't have] patted your bottom." I said, "Is that what he told you?" . . . He had a kid's idea of responsibility for his actions. He had whittled it down with time. . . . It wasn't anything criminal but I wasn't sure I could stop it and I wasn't sure how far it would escalate.

Gaining Control with the Support of the Group

In both the previous incident and in the episode of the actress who reported overtime infractions to the union, effective resolution of problems was reached by using forms of group support. Against the personal attack of the producer, the actress responded as a union deputy monitoring work rules and reporting procedures. In moving the conflict from the personal to the professional level, as the representative of the union, she presented the producer with a larger adversary than he had anticipated.

In the incident of sexual harassment, when confronting the man individually did not help, the actress made his secretive behavior public knowledge bringing him into confrontation with other members of the cast. Their group support gave her a sense of security while she still had to perform with him. She had gained some measure of control over the situation by opening the secret. Finally, she was able to face him and accept his apology. She was also able to tell him that his actions had made friendship between them impossible.

Confrontation is not a choice that women usually make. But in both of these cases, it proved to be an effective strategy. In these instances, each actress found the support she needed was there when she asked for it. In a recent study of the larger society, a large percentage of women were reported to choose conciliation or giving in during stressful situations to avoid confrontation. In contrast, men more often choose confrontation as a means of settling disputes. It is possible that the two actresses who chose confrontation to resolve their problems did so because they are extraordinary women. It is also possible that they chose to resolve their problems in this manner because they are actresses.

Women who choose the profession of acting choose it partly because they are attracted to the element of risk embedded in the exploration of the creative process in themselves and at the level of the group. They are also attracted to the element of risk embedded in the situation of conflict that is the heart of dramatic literature. Learning to work on stage with other performers entails learning to step into a situation where conflicting ideas and desires are taken from the pages of the script and charged with the energy of real people who are determined to have what they want. A beginning actress calls this "stepping into the aura" and she is surprised at how much it costs her in terms of energy to learn to do this. This is a crucial part of the interaction that I see between the work of the performer on stage and the solutions that can be found in similar real situations. It is a subject I would like to return to in the next chapter.

An actress suggests that since there is a less judgmental attitude in the theater towards sexual preference, men may also suffer harassment. Men, especially those who look very young, describe having to make their sexual preference clear to fellow performers, but as one actor says, "There are definite and polite ways to do this." Men do not appear to have the same difficulties with harassment in the theater that women experience. Part of the reason for this may be that in relationships between two men, there is a more even distribution of power. The invitation is not coercive. There are no elements of covertness or entrapment. An actor describes his experience with episodes of this kind.

Men deal with men in a different way. You can tell when a director or somebody you know is kind of feeling the ground. You can feel that kind of energy going on until it's clear [sexual preference], in any way that you make it clear, talking about an old girlfriend or something. It disappears after that. They're used to picking up that kind of hint. There's a click in the head and then you're just a friend. Men are different when they deal with women.

Men are accustomed to making the aggressive response in relationships. According to informants, if they choose to say no, they can do so clearly and forcefully and the message will be accepted. When a woman says no, many men appear to assume she does not mean it. As an actress said, "I didn't know if I could stop it and I didn't know how far it would escalate."

Getting Help from the Union

Both SAG and Equity maintain committees to address the specific concerns of women members. The fall 1987 issue of the Screen Actor Guild's magazine spoke to those concerns in a clear statement of unequal pay. The issue contained a study of the average annual earnings of SAG members by age and sex. Average SAG earnings for members of all ages and both sexes for 1986 were $10,399. Women's average earnings ($7,684) were 26 percent below the general average. In contrast, men's average earnings ($12,433) were 20 percent above. The only age group in which females made more money than males was that of children below the age of ten. I found myself wondering if this means that most babies in television commercials are girls. The study also found that 34 percent or one-third of SAG women had no earnings at all. One-quarter or 27 percent of SAG men had no earnings.

Included with the statistics was a list of strategies the film union is currently pursuing to improve the job opportunities and working conditions for member actresses. Casting reports are required for every production contract so that hiring practices can be reviewed. Meetings are scheduled with network executives to evaluate and promote more opportunities and more realistic portrayals of older women and ethnic minorities (Screen Actor 1987, 26:19).

Men do 90 percent of voice-over commercials because the advertising industry assumes that the male voice carries more authority. Using market research tools that prove the female voice is equally effective in advertising, SAG has targeted advertisers to promote more opportunities for actresses in lucrative voice-over work. Professional counselors offer workshops in combatting sexual harassment at auditions, interviews, and on the set. Advice on how to pursue any necessary legal action is offered (Blake 1987, 18–19). The program described is a positive, affirmative-action approach to equalizing opportunities for women in the profession. Whether or not these strategies achieve substantial gains for women, this activist approach by the union, with its emphasis on sharing information, helps actresses in two additional ways. It publicly recognizes and gives dimensions to the problems experienced by women. At the same time, it encourages in its forceful expression of support the idea that women are indeed entitled to equal treatment. The Guild support is particularly important to women in a profession where the work is often transient and short-term, where female performers often find themselves in the minority and coworkers may be strangers.

In the city of Washington, SAG is usually the first union that performers join. At least a dozen major films have been done in the city every year over the past five years. Rates for day-players and principals constitute good money for performers who work on stage. Film union health and welfare benefits are more comprehensive and more generous than with Equity's program. Since many performers belong to both Equity and Screen Actors Guild, the more activist, financially-empowered SAG can encourage those people who work on stage as well, albeit indirectly. Individual members of the more affluent Screen Actors Guild may respond to encouragement and support from the film union which they then carry into other situations and circumstances when they work on stage.

THREE

STEPPING INTO THE AURA

A lot of actors I work with have an aura that is always with them, that doesn't really change its size from life to the theater. It always stays the same size (which is about five feet from their body in any direction). ... They don't ever exclude it. It has a great deal to do with a power that they use in their lives all the time. If you were to meet me or my fellow actresses, you would not know that we were in theater except for a little more expressiveness. Because I'm afraid to take that power of the aura into my life. I'm afraid people won't believe me. Someone will call my bluff and say, that's not a valid way to be. You're just putting on an act, wearing a persona. It's not you.

I find a lot of actors I know say things, both in life and on stage, to be heard by everyone. They are not timid in any way. Therefore, when you are onstage with them, you must command your own space. It's as if you were in the army in training camp—he did fifty push-ups, you do fifty push-ups. It doesn't matter that he's been doing them since he was twelve and you started four months ago. If I want to be seen in the play, if I want to keep the balance of what's being said in an actual interchange, I have to be very sharp. It's not speaking louder or anything like that ... it's being an active respondent.

Irrespective of me, that actor will continue anyway. It happens more rhythmically than anything else and you begin to match each other. If you want a certain quality to prevail ... you say, I think this scene is really more intimate. So what if we tried it [another way].

I notice in life, men expect, and therefore direct their speech to be heard and society at large has that expectation, too. They expect to hear men before women and that carries over onto the stage.

45

The interaction between life and work on stage that validates and reinforces masculine presence and authority is very specifically described by this actress in talking about her first job in a resident company after she finished her BFA degree. Men, she observes, have a more powerful voice in society than women and that carries over in the theater, not only in the literature but in the personal assurance and authority of actors with whom she works. This general statement may or may not apply to all men everywhere or even all actors. But it is her observation. It describes a pattern of behavior for a group of men with whom this actress works.

An equally important concept that is less specifically stated in her description is that in accepting the challenge of stepping into "the aura," and working on stage with this group of actors, she is forced to craft an equally powerful voice to effectively fill her role in the play. Competition among young actresses is such that if she does not learn to do so, she will not long be a member of the company. She must generate an equally confident presence in order to "keep the balance" of whatever situation is represented in the play. She must convince the audience that she has equal claim to their attention.

The demands of the work call upon her developing skills as an actress. At the same time, they call upon her to reexamine her observation of what audiences and society expect of men and what they expect of women.

She uses an aggressive analogy to express how unfair she feels this to be: "He did fifty push-ups, you do fifty push-ups. It doesn't matter that he's been doing them since he was twelve and you started four months ago." The expectation may be unfair. The effect may be difficult to achieve. But that is what is required by the nature of performance. Whatever it costs in terms of stretching the imaginative construction of who the character is in relation to who she is, whatever time it takes to learn to focus and concentrate levels of performance energies, if she wants to work on stage, she must develop a similar degree of assertive confidence in her performance capabilities that contributes to the quality of presence. In doing so, she is changing a stereotype she has observed and possibly altering the perception of that model of social reality for the audience as well.

A director who understands the performer's process suggests the liberating possibilities that can be available to women in theater.

> It may be that it's an outlet for getting out of the box of being brought up as a woman and feeling certain pressures within the

Diane Defoe, Tamlyn Tomita, Marissa Chibas, and John Gould Rubin in *Don Juan: A Meditation*. Photographer: Jay Thompson. Courtesy of the Mark Taper Forum.

society seeking to define [women] in a subservient or limiting role. In being an actress, the fantasy is very powerful. You get to express your feelings in a way you can't in society. . . . Socially-defined role models [can be] put up for examination and dismembered in the theater.

Depending on temperament, training, and experience, actresses perceive the challenge of performance in different ways. An actress in a university theater program after a season with an Equity company describes her response to age, gender, and developmental differences in the challenge of conflict in a scene.

My nature is to be hesitant to fight back as aggressively. There are things in me that became stronger last year when I was working. I had to get along with everyone.... Being eight years younger than everyone else, I didn't want to be the obnoxious young person.

There's something in me that grew last year trying to keep peace-making. I would think of other ways to come back, probably with the same type of energy but there's something in me that wants to work around it, to fit it, to complement it.

At school, there's a wonderful kid from performance arts who's terribly bold and aggressive. Before I knew him, I didn't want to do a scene with him until I got comfortable. But we had a wonderful scene because it was one of the times when I came back with the energy.

An actress in her thirties who has been working for a number of years says, "Stepping into that masculine energy.... I love doing that. Throwing down the gauntlet. I love a sense of muscularity and physicality in the acting. I love playing to strength. It's sort of sexual and muscular. It's a risk I like taking."

Conflict, confrontation, and competition are dramatic devices that shape the action of most plays. If, as one director says, men may be drawn to acting because it is a nonthreatening way of exploring feelings because there are no irrevocable acts, perhaps women who chose acting do so because they are attracted to those elements of risk inherent in the process of performance.

What women have to say about the things they learn in the process spill back and forth between who they are and how they represent the women they stretch themselves to find in the course of their work. Their comments indicate that the process of stepping into "the aura" of the heightened performance energies of a play can be a significant mechanism for growth and change.

A mature actress who also teaches says, "It's very hard because what you're really doing is exploring the possibilities in yourself. All attitudes are available to you as a person. It's hard to use your own not so nice needs or feelings or let them be exposed without choosing the cop-out of pretending that's not you. It's psychologically and physically wearing." In this kind of exploration, the actress can confront those feelings of anger, egotism, and competitiveness that women are often trained to repress. The actress adds, "You're not wallowing in it, it's done within the larger context" of understanding motives as seen from the inside and showing the audience why this character does what she does.

Learning to "command your space" onstage may have less to do with maturity than experience. An actress who began her career after she already had a professional life and a family describes having to learn to fight for her character's voice in the play. A woman director she was working with reminded her that regardless of the size of her role, she didn't need to feel that she was only taking up time in the play. The author meant her to be there. The audience needed to hear what she had to say. She had not realized that she appeared so hesitant onstage. She says, "I've learned to be rude, to not apologize for taking my turn. I've learned in life from the stage – you sit back there and wait your turn and you won't get the attention that you should have."

Often when actresses talk about how they learn to hold their own in playing a scene, they talk about language as a physical entity that must be structured. Breath control, pausing, rhythm, emphasis, voice production are elements that function to illuminate and give dramatic effect to the words supplied by the playwright. In the following description, another young actress describes the difficulties she experienced in learning to hold up her end of a scene where she played a visitor intruding on a couple in the middle of a shouting match.

She realized from the beginning that she did not have the vocal control to match that of the other two performers. But she was surprised to find that they could get the scene working if she took out the pauses she thought she had to make. Originally, she took the actor's suggestion in rehearsal because of his experience. Then she developed a real respect for his advice when she discovered a key to making the scene effective.

> That is their scene and I intrude on it. It's so high energy. I don't have the kind of control I need over my breath yet to hold my own in that scene.... [The actor playing the husband] would say, you can't pause there, you're holding everything up. I just thought, OK, this guy's done a lot of theater. I'll take the pause out and see what happens and he was right every time. So then I started going to him and it's gotten a lot better.
>
> You have to go in ... and match it. I could damage the scene. It shouldn't be two points and then a lower point. It should be three points of frenetic energy.
>
> It's hard because in that scene, you feel unwanted anyway. You feel it the whole time. There was a part of me that felt like I had walked in on a married couple in a fight. You do have to get as tough as they are. What I found was that they appreciated it once the scene was really working.

She talks about the unease over feeling not wanted as being quite real even though this is an imaginary situation in a play between three performers who are acting. The effort that it took to overcome these feelings was a surprise to her, but it was what the scene required. It is what fuels the tension in what becomes a three-way struggle.

> I found you can't say, but I don't like that kind of thing. If it's called for, it's called for. You have to make those leaps. When you take the risk and you let it be free, you're OK. You've done your work in rehearsal. That allows you to listen as though you're hearing it not for the first time, but you can forget that you heard it before.

Theories of ensemble acting are sometimes expressed in terms of group support, in performers giving to each other on stage. But actors who have spent a number of years in resident companies feel this is a misconception of ensemble playing. "That's not what the audience came to see." They describe the dynamics of working together in a much more aggressive manner.

> If you're relaxed and you're trying to achieve some kind of communion out there, that means you're alert to what's going on in their face and in their body.... If a question is asked of you, you're alert to them. There are little tricks and accidents that you can cause to happen which will really bring you back to being there with the other person.... The only thing that makes me know I exist is you. If you're not there, if I don't see you there, I don't exist. You're the thing that's making me. So the more you demand of me, the more I demand of you, the better it works.

Another actor who also teaches develops a similar theory of the dynamics of performance. He notes that in workshop and class discussions, women are initially less comfortable with the opportunism of this approach than men.

> There are a lot of forces at work. When you take on a role, you do take on a life, and there are a number of forces that are determined to use that life for their own ends—the playwright, the director, other actors, the audience. They all have their own connections to that life and they want to use that life to fill those connections. . . . We are in fact inseparable, all of us—audience, actors, director, playwright.
> When I look at all the different forces that can want to use the role, in each instance, I find that everybody who is trying to use that

Pamela Reed and Joe Morten in *Elektra* by Ezra Pound. Photographer: Paula Cort. Courtesy of CSC Repertory.

life is in turn usable by that life. And then it comes down to the fact that the one most greedy is the one most usable.

What's going on there isn't real and one of the most unreal things about it is the conflict itself ... the people who seem to be so set against one another are really working together. But the illusion that they are working against one another is the fundamental and crucial relation. I find the more I am attuned to that relation, the more effective I can be in my [ability to manipulate] what the audience choses to think.

Language and behavior as tools of performance are described in these comments from the point of view of the people who use them. This theory of performance may well appear Machiavellian to people outside the theater. However, the actor's understanding of the nature of conflict represented in the play demands the aggressive opposition of performers involved in that conflict. The demands are the same for both men and women. "The respect is in the work." The audience is more involved and the illusion of the play is more effective if the men and women who struggle with each other on stage are represented by the performers as equal adversaries. Understood in these terms, it is the nature of performance that requires an equally powerful voice for men and women.

The Quality of Presence

A number of references, "the power of the aura," "wearing a persona," "command your space," embedded in the first long account in this chapter can be understood as descriptions of the quality of presence onstage. In terms of stagecraft, this is a beginning actress talking about the difficulties of learning to confront performance energies in fellow actors that are more developed than her own.

Other performers, both men and women, recognize the aura described as stage presence that commands attention. It can be fueled by a variety of different energy sources: a quality of personal magnetism, sexuality, extraordinary physical or vocal gifts, depth of concentration, or the capacity to make some direct connection with the play or the audience or another performer. Special qualities of presence are part of the performer's abilities. They can spill over into life but they do not necessarily do so.

The young actress observes that men have a more powerful voice in society than women. But just as all men do not conform to the stereotype of the male authority figure – they may lack confidence, decisiveness, judgment, etc. – so all actors do not possess remarkable qualities of presence when they begin their careers. And they may be only minimally aware of the presence they generate as they acquire more experience. Somewhere in the many newspaper tributes to Laurence Olivier after his death, I remember reading that even after the general public recognized his considerable accomplishments, he still sometimes thought of himself as "walking around in his father's oversize shoes."

I think of two actors I have watched continually over the last 25 years and remember that one began in funny fat man parts where he took out his teeth and whistled his s's. The other played nervous juveniles with knees that refused to work right. Straight roles with no character physicalization to hide in were more difficult for both men. They had trouble finding the character or generating a presence in such parts.

Twenty-some years of uninterrupted work on every kind of play imaginable have allowed them to stretch their abilities in a formidable achievement of roles. I don't know in which productions in that long period they acquired the extraordinary qualities of presence they now have. Unlike stars who exhibit their larger than life personalities, they submerge themselves in the role and convince me completely that they are some other person who compels attention as soon as they arrive on stage. When they step into that space, it is as though they have come home.

An actress I have seen off and on over the same period began as an ingenue with a very direct manner, a pretty girl with sharp edges to her personality. After 20 years of regional theater, she makes an enigmatic woman in a Pinter play riveting and her Shaw women invade their drawing rooms with style and wit that glistens like polished crystal. So I know that presence grows with experience and can be, but is not necessarily, easier for men to acquire than women. Since parts for women are often smaller and less challenging in many plays, it would seem reasonable to assume that since they get less time and therefore less experience on stage than men, women might have more difficulty acquiring special qualities. That in fact does not seem to be true. Actors who teach talk about the number of good actresses they see in their classes, often with more talent and better skills than the men. An actor with many years of experience points out

> There are men and women who have an aura that is outgoing. You can see it from across the stage and it's very exciting to play with. There was a physical one with [an actor with whom he played *Lear*]. It was the power of his voice. He may even have been suffering from emphysema. We were in robes and leather. He could hit a tone, and you would feel it tap the leather on your chest across the stage.

He adds, "Of course, it means rising to an occasion." He mentions a young actor with whom he worked over the past year. "He gave off an incredible magnetism. It was potentially intimidating. There was a sensation of fear, a physical sensation." He remembers reminding himself in early rehearsals, "he can't hurt me."

Physical size does not in itself establish an actor's presence onstage, but it can reinforce those qualities already there and make confrontation formidable for men as well as women. An actor talks about the difficulties he has with another man with whom he is often cast.

> There's an actor in town who is similar in size. We've often played brothers, cousins, father and son. He gets lots of awards. He's a powerful actor and he has that space around him. Now I'm lucky, I'm a large man. I know that I'm going to have to deal with him confrontationally. But that usually works for the play. That's usually what the play is about, that confrontation. I can see it would be very

difficult for a woman. . . . The last show I did with him, the only way
he had of playing a love scene was to overpower the woman.

A young actor talks about a potentially intimidating scene he
had to play with a mature actor. Both the preparation of this scene
and the performance of it had the value of being a tremendous learning experience for him.

His powers of observation are quite extraordinary as they are
manifested in his acting. [In the scene they played] . . . he was
watching me to see whether he could detect the smell of a lie. I decided that I was going to play the scene as though it were truthful
which was not out of character because I had decided this man was
a psychopath. So it was possible for me to believe everything I was
saying, at least in the moment.
  Because the scene led to aggression, it did have that quality. I was
cognizant of trying to manipulate the other actor with my words.
It was the best scene I ever did, only because I was prepared and
I was capable of dealing with that energy. It could be potentially intimidating but [in that scene] it wasn't. It was great!

Performance energy can also be fueled by the actress or the actor discovering that they themselves share some intensely felt idea
with the character they are playing. In playing Georgie, the wife of
a troubled actor in *The Country Girl*, an actress found in the middle
of performance that

what the character was struggling with, I was also struggling with.
. . . I suddenly observed that about myself. . . . Georgie was so
jealous of his talent and made him need her. . . . While he was going
on about himself, I was doing my interior tape of "you talk a lot
about yourself; don't you ever get tired of talking about yourself"
and I realized those were my thoughts as well as Georgie's.
  Most actors are narcissistic. They have to be. They're paid to be.
I accept that but I still don't like it. I often feel that about men actors. They have power. They're more desired. All theaters want
them. . . . I've been lucky. I've worked a lot and gotten good
reviews. . . . But I still want to be as powerful as him. . . . It's like
when you're growing up as a girl, at some point you realize boys
have more fun.

"The Imperfect Actor"

As some of the previous comments of performers indicate, for a
performance to be relaxed and effortless (as it appears to the au-

dience), performance energies must be focused and controlled but they can not be forced. Relaxing, to most of us, means doing nothing. It can also mean to be free of tension, to be open to whatever happens from moment to moment, to have no agenda of what must be accomplished for a certain space of time. It is in this sense that the performer talks about relaxing and letting the part come. It is difficult for people who don't work on stage to understand how anyone can relax and still maintain the levels of energy necessary for performance.

An actress who has spent 40 years in the theater describes the extreme state into which performers can put themselves when they haven't yet learned to trust their creative process.

I was in a very demanding part.... I'm better at that now forty years later but I wasn't in the very beginning. If I didn't feel I was slipping into this little keyhole where the part is and I didn't feel the natural rush of inspiration, I would think, Oh God, it's going to be a flat performance.

So instead of relaxing and finding it that way (which you do, you don't find it by forcing it out of you), I was forcing everything.

There was one scene towards the end of the first act where somebody asked my character a question and I get faint and fall to my knees beside this little bench. So I fell to my knees beside the little bench and thought, this is very effective. I'm doing this well. And the next thing I heard was a groan from the audience. ... and the actor behind me said my name under his breath. And I thought, what's happened? Are my trousers split? What could have happened?

Then [the character had no lines] for a few minutes. The actors around me were talking. And I felt something dropping on my hands, something wet. And I thought, the theater's leaking. It's raining and the theater's leaking. I heard my cue and stood up and when I looked down, there was this deluge of blood over everything, over the front of my costume, on the floor in front of me.

I thought, where is that coming from? I put my hand to my mouth and my lip was smashed. I had fallen and hit the edge of the stool and didn't realize it. Didn't feel anything. That was how hard I was trying. I smashed the lip open, smashed the inside of my mouth. Blood was just gushing out. So I covered my mouth with my hand, and went downstage to act the next scene with [another actor]. He was a big strong man but he got white as paper. I put my back to the audience and took hold of his arm and we finished the scene. The stage manager, who could see what had happened, took down the curtain and brought me backstage to put ice on it and I went on.

But that was an accident of my own making. I was trying too

hard. It was a big lesson. That's how far I was away from myself. Shakespeare has a wonderful sonnet about the actor who is "beside himself," the imperfect actor.

"The Imperfect Actor" as a Hazard to the Group

"When you're in a high emotional state, some people get carried away and I don't like being hit. So I make sure that that won't happen."

When a performer is on the losing end of a fight onstage, it is difficult not to anticipate what is going to happen night after night. No one looks forward to taking a slap on a regular basis. The best protection that performers have is that in most instances, any scene involving physical violence is choreographed move by move in careful sequence so that everyone knows what to expect and no one is out of control in the emotion of the moment. In some Shakespearean theaters, because of the danger of swordplay, the fight sequences are rehearsed every night before the performance. Still, an actor counts his sword wounds and says, "It's like the travails of St. Paul."

There is a story that no matter how many westerns he did, John Wayne would not accept a gun from the special prop man on a film set unless it was handed to him in the correct way. He was never casual about weapons. In contrast, an actress remembers going out in the back alley behind the theater in Boston and shooting off bunches of blanks to learn to handle the old-fashioned pistols she had to use in *Hedda Gabler*. In the course of the run, she got over her fear of the guns but still got powder burns on her hands until closing night.

Although most performers take very seriously their responsibilities to each other, if an actress has a bad experience, she can find it difficult to trust the next situation completely. "If you're trusting another actor," someone says, "and you don't feel completely safe with them, that makes you get afraid. . . . I've never been terribly wounded but it's the feeling of violation of trust. It threw me out of the play."

She describes the strategy she used to gain more control over her situation in playing several scenes with an actor in which he was required to slap her. She asked him to meet her in the green room

and go through the choreography for the scene before every performance. This had the double advantage of rehearsing the moves and
allowing her to meet and talk with him backstage before she had to
meet him in character within the violent framework of the scenes
they played together. She explained that she was less afraid of being
hurt than of "being thrown out of the play," of losing her concentration and her credibility in the life of the play through the physical impact of the slap.

Another actress, working in a tiny theater in New York,
describes just that experience when the actor she was playing with
refused to choreograph their fight scene because he felt it would lose
its spontaneity. During a performance, he did lose control and struck
her hard enough to give her a bloody nose.

> I think my main concern was that the audience would worry about
> me, the actress, as opposed to the character I was playing and then
> the whole thing would be shot. .... What I tried to do was to go on
> to the next moment and not worry about it . . . [but] The next per-
> formance I was so aware of what was happening, I was flinching.
> I wasn't really acting. I was so worried. Every time he put his hand
> up, I would shy away. Once he knew that I was afraid and not able
> to . . . act or really live on stage, he was very good about it. [But]
> he wouldn't choreograph it. He refused to. He just didn't touch me
> so therefore we had a stagnant scene that didn't work.

I don't want to suggest that only actresses risk real violence
when their scene partners lose control or lack the technical discipline
to be precise in their actions night after night. I remember a deepen-
ing bruise in my husband's chest when the actor who stabbed him
onstage missed the padding almost every night for the six-week run
of the show. In a stock production where a fight scene occurred, I
remember watching the father slam the son's head against a wooden
set piece. The actor playing the boy got up and reeled off in the
wrong direction. Clearly, he did not know for a moment where he
was.

Both actresses and actors describe their concern with safety but
also with preserving the illusion of the play. They see a real act of
sudden unexpected violence as an interruption of that illusion for
themselves and for the audience. They are disappointed in their
stage partner for reasons that have to do with attention to craft, the
discipline of stage technique, and the violation of a relationship of
trust that is part of the shared nature of performance.

Voice, Presence, and the Possibilities
of Performance

The concept of voice can be seen to include language and behavior as well as self-investigation and a knowledge of the larger world. But "presence" remains an elusive quality. It is possible to talk about the various sources of energy that fuel it and the ways that performers interact with it onstage but presence remains a quality that is easier to describe than to define. The student actor can arrive onstage with it or it may be acquired in the course of work. Performers either have some special quality that becomes a focus of attention or they enter and leave the stage capably but without particular notice.

Language and behavior are the nuts and bolts of the profession, but a larger concept of voice implies continuing investigation of self and a curiosity about the world and the human relationships that give context to the playwright's vision. Performers talk about how they attempt to achieve this. An actress points out that "all attitudes are available to you as a person" but it can be difficult to confront the darker qualities in oneself in order to understand and illuminate motivations of character for an audience. These are the unattractive qualities that women are often schooled to repress as children. The process can be physically and psychologically wearing but it is useful both as self-knowledge and in providing an insider's view of character and motivation.

Learning to fight for the character's voice in the play, however small the role, carries over into life situations for an actress who came late into the profession. Twenty years ago many women joined classes in assertiveness training in order to build confidence and to develop a stronger voice for themselves in society. For actresses, assertiveness is learned in performance.

Learning to be an "active respondent" includes deliberately shaping individual vocal qualities to better affect an audience. It also entails learning to structure language using phrasing, rhythm, and emphasis so as to accomplish whatever the action of the play requires. This may be something one would never do in real life, but the actress must be prepared to address strong feelings of aversion and use them in the context of the scene.

These more aggressive attitudes are necessary for the kind of ensemble performance that brings a play fully to life in front of an audience. An actor who has spent most of his career working out this

Carole Meyers and Bill Whitaker in *Scheherazade* by Marisha Chamberlain. Photographer: Richard Batch. Courtesy of Horizons Theater.

theory in a resident company of performers says, "When you take on a role, you take on a life and there are a number of forces that are determined to use that life for their own ends." The crucial relation here is a storm of conflict played out together with an audience who interact with and respond to what they see. "We are in fact inseparable, all of us, audience, actors, director, playwright." This larger view of the group that is created in the act of performance is in itself an asset in learning to work on stage. It can be faced as adversary and at the same time drawn on for support. "We are in fact inseparable." "The more you demand of me, the more I demand of you, the better it works."

Learning how to step into the heightened life of performance is an attractive but not an easy experience for the young actress described at the beginning of this chapter. She observes that men in the company bring to that experience a power that they use in their lives all the time. She gives a number of reasons why she is afraid to take this power into her own life: "People won't believe me ... you're putting on an act, wearing a persona ... it's not you." In the theater and in life, these actors "expect and therefore direct" their speech to be heard. If she wants to keep the balance of what is being said, if she wants to be seen in the play with them, she must be an "active respondent." By stepping into the aura and competing at the same level of performance as the men in the play, she can learn to craft an equally powerful voice that will resonate effectively with the play, the other performers, and the audience. It is her observation that "society expects to hear men before women and that carries over to the theater." But if she is successful in learning her craft, she will have stretched the limits of that expectation both for herself and possibly for the audience. Learning to step into the aura of power that is generated by a group of performers, men or women, who have developed qualities of voice and presence capable of bringing the play to life and drawing the emotions of the audience into the performance can be a powerful impetus for growth and change. Understood in these terms, this experience is a close description of the nature of performance. It has a significant effect on both the men and women who make their lives in it, but particularly, I think, on women.

FOUR

INVESTING IN THE GROUP AND OWNING THE WORK

There is a mutual understanding among the performers interviewed here that the making of a play is a collaborative art. Although there are conditions surrounding any given production that performers recognize as limitations on their individual creativity, they would all agree that in the best of circumstances the group process is one of the reasons they chose to work in theater.

Other arts, writing, painting, sculpture, are solitary but theater depends upon the interaction of individual creativity. What performers enjoy in that interaction appears to be the impetus supplied by several imaginations focused on the creation of the piece, the energy that comes from the shared experience, and the feeling of trust in the group that is working toward a common goal in the making of the play. One actor told me that he set out to be a writer but the whole business was too lonely.

Performers set a particular value on the group interaction of rehearsal. Years ago, most plays were built around star performers or actor-managers who controlled all aspects of their productions. Broadway shows and touring companies of those shows are still built around stars to some extent. However, if those stars are American, they generally share a tradition of training that places considerable value on the dynamics of the rehearsal process. This investigative process may be limited by time or money, enormous yet fragile egos, or differences in technique. Still, one of the reasons performers say they enjoy stage work more than film or television is the exploratory work that the group can do in rehearsal. It is rare for there to be anything that a stage performer can recognize as rehearsal work in the making of films or television. An actor who spent the early part of his career in New York and regional theater describes being so confused by his first experience doing a film comedy that he began to believe there was no film in the camera and the whole project was a tax write-off for somebody's rich relative. The film turned out to be a major success both critically and commercially.

The technology of film and television generally removes the individual performer from contact with the audience. In live theater, the immediate connections that performers make through rehearsal and on stage with the play, each other, the director, and the audience feed their creative intuitions and ideas. These connections also allow them to feel that they are in control of their work. In talking about a theory of performance in the previous chapter, an actor described the bond of relationships between playwright, director, actors, and audience. "We are in fact inseparable," he says. Each one establishes a network of connections with the others. Each one needs something from the others. Paradoxically, the effect of that collaboration for performers when the play works is described by an actress as a feeling of release.

> The shared responsibility I find enormously helpful. The closer one gets to acknowledging that it is a fundamentally shared responsibility to create the piece, the more freeing it is. I'm thinking of the rehearsal process.
> Then the surprise is to bring what you have collectively created to an audience and realize that you've bumped up to the next level of creative experience. . . . Letting go into the collective experience of living is an extraordinary release, an extraordinary loss of burden.

An actor who worked for years in a resident company remembers that he would sometimes come in to do the show and sit down at the dressing table with all of his individual problems in his head — no time for family, lack of money, his future, his health. The last thing he wanted to do was this play. Then, in the course of the performance, all of that would fall away. The depression of the dressing room would be forgotten and he would find his energy renewed in the heightened experience of the shared life of the play.

An actress compares her work onstage to her second career as a clinical social worker, a profession which leaves her feeling drained and exhausted.

I've never played. I don't do that. I was a first child with alcoholic parents. But when I go to the theater, it's work that is rejuvenating. It's invigorating, unlike working with my clients.... I can get [whatever energies are needed] from the theater, I think because there is an element of play there.

A young actor agrees. "It isn't work when you have [an ensemble]. The working off each other is spontaneous and it's exciting." He remembers the tremendous effort it cost him to create the illusion of a blossoming romance in a play without any help from the actress with whom he was paired. She

> was an entity in herself. She didn't want to have anything to do with anyone. She knew what her performance was.... I had to remember the performance I saw [in another production] and pretend to work off that.... It was so much work! I'd come offstage sweating profusely. I always know when I'm working too hard. My clothes are drenched.... The worst kind of play you can do is when everyone is their own person, very individual ... and ungiving.

An actor friend says that he feels that he has always been too concerned with what other people think of him. He worries over his fellow actors, the director's notes, the critics reviews. But there have been for him some memorable performances when he thought of nothing and no one but the life of the play expressed in a tremendous force of energy that seemed to him to come from somewhere beneath the stage, flowing through him like an open column.

Sometimes, because of the atmosphere or the weather or problems in the theater or some event outside it, a performer says, "you feel that you are trying so hard to reach the others onstage but there is no connection. You flail away at the space between you unable to touch anyone." Other times everything, every sound, every gesture, acquires an edge, and performances catch fire from one another until the audience and the performers realize they have been part of something extraordinary.

The most encouraging situation for ensemble playing or artistic collaboration is usually the resident company where people have learned to trust each other and share a common vocabulary that relates to the work. An actress describes the environment of the working rehearsal as a particularly vulnerable one. "When you are in the work situation ... you have to consciously take down all of your screens, all of the filters and protectors that you've spent your life building, consciously make a decision to take that down" and risk whatever comes. The necessary climate of permission can be nurtured or destroyed by any of the participants. Another actress says

> You have to have the familiarity that leads to being able to make a fool of yourself in front of the others because it's not judgmental. The more familiar you are, the easier it is to get to that place where you can make a fool of yourself which I think is the beginning of learning. As long as you're in [that kind of situation] . . . you can find something that works. So I enjoy that, provided they [the others in rehearsal] are also doing the same thing. They're also taking risks.

A director who is accustomed to working in this situation talks about the value of relying on the group in solving the complex problems posed by the play.

> It's an amazing experience when separate energies coalesce on a problem, pass through the prism, and come out as a collective moment. . . . It's not just a stage phenomena. It can happen with a group discussing a problem. I think the Quakers have a wonderful view of the truth, that everybody possesses part . . . and the collective truth will emerge if you let people talk.
>
> You can be discussing a problem and people haven't any point of view and then as you turn it around and ask the right lead questions . . . a solution emerges. I really respect the process . . . and I trust it. I believe that your main job as a creative leader is to bring together the right people and ask the right questions and set up the right circumstances so that the people can evolve and bring out what's best in them, the collective.

The kind of discussion that is described here is focused on the specifics of the play that is being done. Its purpose is the examination of the play in question, not the fostering of closer working relationships within the group. There are directors who use theater games in early rehearsals to build an ensemble feeling, a strategy that a young actor complains about as a waste of time.

> Some directors [think] my play won't be good unless everyone is friendly with each other and everyone gets along. A lot of the first week of the rehearsal process that should be spent on blocking is spent on theater games that are supposed to meld this group into an ensemble. I hate that. It's a waste of time. It'll either happen or it won't.

This is a fairly common complaint among performers who see

improvisation used in this way as a waste or an inefficient use of rehearsal time. Many kinds of associations, businesses, and professional groups have learned to use improvisational games as a means of establishing an atmosphere of relaxation and informality among their members. Theater games are often used differently by performers. For them, improvisation can be a kind of intuitive thought process that they use to explore a range of possibilities which can be useful in making specific choices in a role.

A director also talks about the drawbacks of the investigative rehearsal process for directors.

> There are moments when you're the enemy and those are always uncomfortable. You just have to get through those. You're not always popular leading a group process. Individual needs can butt up against each other and you're supposed to resolve them and you really may not "know" how. Yeah. It's uncomfortable. You're on the line. It's not like writing a poem or watching television. It's not private, it's public. The public process is difficult.

When directors give only lip service to the capabilities of the group or impose a structure that severely limits collaboration, performers are likely to view them as natural adversaries. An actress complains, "Directors are a hot topic in this business. The current vogue is that it's a director's theater. It's not ours. And that's not very helpful. They create obstacles and they have to be present all the time."

In reading a biography of Katharine Cornell, a performer is surprised to learn that only during Cornell's career did directors begin to occupy the central position of influence from which they can choose not to allow the group to investigate the play and rigidly impose their own views on the individual performer. Even in the resident company, a director coming in to recreate a production he has previously done elsewhere can limit individual expression. A director with an appreciation of how actors work says

> It comes down to a question of ownership of the work. The actor has to believe they own the moment on stage. They've given life to it. It's theirs. In some cases, it's clear that the moment was discovered, created by them, even though they may have been guided to it by the director or another actor in rehearsal. It's easy for them from night to night to enter it and just be there. Or they feel particularly connected with another performer or with an audience. The work has a presence acknowledged between them and the audience.

In shows where the director has come in and just "put it on" the
company, and stifled a lot of individual creativity, the shows have
been very successful but what the actor's work becomes is just that:
fulfilling a set of obligations which are outside of his own sense of
life. They [the actors] put a great deal of concentration and energy
into the accomplishment of a task which is never transformed. The
task never disappears and becomes something more.

Descriptions of how the work done in rehearsal can be transformed during the process of performance to a creative experience
helps make understandable the disaffection that performers harbor
for directors who insist on controlling every creative decision that a
performer makes to build a role. The actor may then find that he or
she is working very hard but that the character never fully comes to
life. The audience may not see the difference but the performer is
aware of it.

One reason that directors may not know more than they do
about the actor's creative process is that a fair number of performers
do not like to talk about what they are doing. They may feel that
creative energy is dissipated in talking away ideas before the
underlying behavior is set in place or that they think best on their
feet or that they need to use the critical eye of the director in a certain way. An actor says

> I don't believe in talking a lot to a director about what is happening.
> My fear is that if I explain it all to him, he understands what I'm
> about and sees what I'm doing. Well, he sees it because he's been
> informed. So I'd rather not inform him and then he sees it or he
> doesn't, and then he can tell me what he sees. So I don't like a lot
> of talking.

On the other hand, the experience of a freewheeling give and
take between playwright, director, actors, and actresses in a small
company is a truly valuable experience for a young actress.

> If you have a suggestion to make, he [the director] . . . will actually
> scribble it down. It's a group project. Everyone works on it. It's
> because we have a writer in the group and directors . . . we can say
> certain things, even about the plays we pick. I can say, "You've
> rewritten this woman and she's nothing but a sex maniac. What
> have you been reading lately, Anais Nin?" And he says, "No, I meant
> her to do this and she wants to kill this man because—" It's a real
> interchange.

Someone else points out that the performer may not agree with a director's notes. He or she may resent the criticism but what the director says is going to be there in one's mind. It's difficult to kill an idea. If the idea is good, then the next night or two nights or two weeks later, that idea may click into place and the performance will take off and begin to soar. So one can't afford to be unavailable to the director's ideas. Actors collect bits and pieces of everyone they have ever met. They can't afford to close themselves off to ideas or to what the director's eye sees during the rehearsal process.

Sometimes a director's interpretation of a play can be so constricting that basic survival instincts erupt from performers. Faced with week after week of a mountain of detailed notes on his developing performance, a seasoned character actor describes how he finally fell into a full-throated rage in rehearsal and had to go off to the men's room to calm down.

In another kind of power struggle, an actress talks about her difficulties with a director's view of the two female characters in *Titus Andronicus*.

The play is not one of Shakespeare's best. People feel that the characters are not written with three dimensions but I was determined to make Tamara a full woman, not just a villain.

The story is that Titus slaughters her son needlessly after the war is over as a ritual sacrifice to the spirits of all of his sons who have died. It's stupid, unnecessary slaughter and then that is the reason Tamara does all the awful things she does: the rape and mutilation of Titus' daughter Lavinia and the killing of his two sons.

The director was not at all interested, in fact, took great offense whenever I tried to bring a three-dimensional quality to this woman. He just wanted her to be a cartoon image. He just wanted villainy. That's all. Anytime I brought up the possibility that this was a person who was reacting to being hurt and this was the only way she knew to strike back, it was unwanted by him. We had huge arguments.

The girl playing Lavinia also was confronted and slapped down every time she tried to get a voice going in the play. She was directed with her back to the audience most of the time. You were rarely able to see her face. He cut most of her lines. Lavinia has a wonderful interchange in the beginning of the play and she's got a nice long scene with Tamara. But he was afraid that the way the role was written, she was too shrewish and that the audience would be saying, go ahead: kill her, rape her, mutilate her. He had no room in his mind for possibilities. He just saw her as a shrew and therefore she should be raped.

[With Tamara], he couldn't allow that the killing of her firstborn

son would make her seek revenge, and yet he allowed Titus full
humanity. Every time that actor would come in with a choice,
something that would help him get from A to B to C, that was acceptable. All the men basically were allowed to have full [characteriza-
tions]. The two women around whom the story revolves were not
allowed that.

I didn't behave well with it. For a while in rehearsal I did manage
to hold my own and say, let me find the dignity here. I think it's more
chilling if someone sees the light and goes to darkness instead. Let
me investigate the motherhood in this woman and . . . find out what
it costs her to do brutal things. I think that's where the tragedy lies.
It's more arresting to see evil wrestle with light. Well, he wouldn't
hear of it.

Finally, it ended up with me stamping my feet and . . . shouting
out "let me breathe." It just popped out of me. He threw a . . . fit
and that was the end of our communication. All of the notes he had
for me would go through his assistant director, this woman whom
he felt was the only person who could talk to me. He just dropped
talking to me. That was it. He just left me.

I was willing to duke it out with him. I thought I was being clean
with my anger. . . . I felt like I was fighting for my life. I didn't want
to do any representation of women that wasn't honest. I agreed that
what Tamara does isn't right but I wanted to show why. I wanted
there to be a living human being there. Lavinia was caught in the
same thing. She did not want to be a victim. He said to the assistant
director, and she passed it on to me, that he believed in ultimate
figures of good and evil. His vision of the world was that way. But
I also think it had to do with the fact that he had no idea of what
women were about. . . .

The irony was that we opened and I did my best to follow his direction. I thought, well, all right. I'm going to give him the benefit of
the doubt. I'll follow his direction. The reviews from that night on
me were . . . that it was a bland performance. . . . I didn't read the
reviews until after the show [closed].

After opening, I remember thinking, OK, now that he's gone, I am
going to take this role back to myself and I inserted all the humanity. I put back all the decisions . . . that everything costs her. . . .
There was a critic who had come a week later and saw that performance. In that review, there was a paragraph [applauding the range
and quality of the performance] . . . and I know that he saw me doing my work, not just the director's.

I feel bad about that not so much for the reviews but for that
character and for womenkind. . . . I want to say to him, how dare
you make a decision about humanity and about women. . . . He had
seen [another production] of *Titus* that had [impressed] him.
Basically our production was his tribute to that version.

In the interviews, one often-suggested solution to this kind of fundamental conflict is that more women should seek positions of power as directors and producers. In Washington, there are already a number of women who have established theaters where they also direct. Most performers have no strong gender preferences with regard to directors. Women may have the same talents or flaws as men. Either sex is capable of abusing the powers held by the director. What performers do appreciate in any director is organization, respect for the actor's process, and an investigative rehearsal atmosphere.

The process of reeducation toward equality of the sexes that is generally operative in American society is also evident in the theater. The impetus for change comes most directly from younger women, both Black and white, who are educated to expect equal status or who have spent some part of their personal lives struggling for it. These women indicate that there is a price to pay for speaking up on this issue in the theater. There is an older male hierarchy of power in both the artistic and commercial theater that expects the young to be seen and not heard. Young men as well as women can feel put down by this group. But since there are fewer opportunities for and greater competition among actresses the consequences of losing a job are more serious.

An actor recalls a director's condescending treatment of young actresses and suggests how difficult it is to change such attitudes when they represent the habits of a lifetime. "Why don't you learn to deal differently with women? Why don't you learn to speak Spanish in five minutes?"

An actress uses the phrase "own the role" and describes a situation in which the director did not allow that.

> [He had] a way of working that I'm unfamiliar with. He would basically tell me where he wanted me to stand, where he wanted the angle of my head. I felt like a puppet. There were certain actors that were able to bring life to that strict discipline structure. For me, it was like beating a horse. All my impulses were not used, were not appropriate to what he physically wanted. So there was no communication.
>
> It was very degrading, dehumanizing. I noticed that I would say to people, "come see the play I'm in" as opposed to "come see my play." It's a semantic thing but it made me realize that when a director leaves, it becomes my play as opposed to this thing that I am doing for someone else.
>
> It was educating, working with him, painful as it was. On a personal level, I learned where my limits are as an artist. When you're

an actor, you're in a very vulnerable situation. . . . You're willing to give anything. You put your trust in directors, expecting that you're working for the same end result . . . and when that's violated, it's really devastating. . . . I just kept working. I don't think I gave him the best performance I'm capable of and I didn't feel he got what he wanted from me so if I had to do it again, I would confront him and say, you can't talk to me this way. I can't work with you. We'll have to find another way to communicate with each other. Or I would say, you'll have to find another actress.

I'd never dealt with that situation. . . . I'd never experienced sexism like that. That was sort of a battle that my mother fought. I really never have had to deal with being discriminated against because I'm a woman. He treated me and the other younger women in the company differently. He treated the older women with a deference, not the way he treated the men – which was with mutual respect, as equal human beings.

His attitude toward me and [another young actress] was really condescending, sort of, "You're a young woman and you should be honored to be in the same room with me." And I was [assuming], "We're doing a play together, we're artists. You have more experience than me but I have a lot to offer as well and I can do things on stage you can't. We can learn from each other." That has always been the way I've felt with other actors on stage, even when they've had many more years of experience. I'm not intimidated by them. I have a lot to offer and they can learn from me. It's always a two-way street. That's why I'm in this work. It's a collaborative effort. [But in this instance] we were just coming from different worlds.

Difficult directors, no matter how tightly they control rehearsals, can still be outmaneuvered. Another actress describes how she worked at a similar situation. She used the advantage of observing the rehearsals before she had to work with the director in question.

I watched [how he worked] with some of the other women first. He put them through a pretty bad time, some of them. I decided that I was going to come into the first rehearsal with the lines down [something not all actors like to do because it can limit the performance in various ways].

He went to great lengths to describe the scene . . . what he wanted this woman to do. I said, that doesn't make sense. . . . I'll try it your way but it doesn't ring true at all. He shrugged and announced he was going to do that act without stopping. I thought, now's my chance and I changed everything.

It worked because I had thought through an alternative and was off book. I presented him with a fait accompli and he liked it. If I was still on book, he would have had the advantage. He had tremendous energy and could talk you under the table.

When the director imposes on the performer's process in rehearsal, he or she violates a bond of trust that the performer may have made with the group. Someone says, "when you are in the work situation, you are essentially powerless because . . . you have to consciously take down all of your logical screens, all of the filters and protectors that you've spent your life building." In that state of openness, the performer is a vulnerable target for whoever choses to impose on the situation.

Most performers respect each other's process in rehearsal and give no suggestions or advice to anyone unless they are specifically asked. Those who violate the rule and make premature judgments on someone's performance risk damaging the rehearsal process for everyone. "You can always tell when someone's stepping out [of their character] and doing your work because he's a frustrated director," says a gifted 25-year-old actress speaking of her experience with an actor who wanted "to teach acting lessons" in rehearsal. "He would say things like, you know what I was thinking? You know that part? Maybe you could—" Although she kept her temper and fed her anger into the scene, what she wanted to say to him was, "I don't know the character. I'm trying to figure her out, but my process is my process and none of your business. . . . Leave my work alone! You do your work, damn it!"

Apparently, being a young woman posed a number of hazards in that production. The strategy she used to avoid problems showed considerable restraint and an understanding of the advantages of formality that is impressive for someone in their twenties.

> I would not for a second let them see that they're getting to me. You've got to hold your own, especially if you're a woman . . . and then being young. Then they treat you like you don't know anything in the first place.
>
> But see, if you say something [it interferes with the work]. If you just say, I'll think about that and walk away, that's better than making rifts in the cast early on. I've seen that happen and it makes things treacherous. You can't get over it. People will be never forgetting, people with egos like that. It's so ugly, and you can't get work done because you're thinking not about the scene but what that idiot's doing.
>
> I ignored it, acted like I was oblivious to it. At the same time, what you do is you isolate yourself from the other people. I'd come to rehearsal, talk to people I wanted to talk to, be cordial with everyone else and then leave. . . . I put on armor to go to rehearsal and you shouldn't have to work that way. But you have to learn how

to work that way, I guess, in case it does come up. Obviously, there are people like that.

A Black actress talks about the stages she went through as she learned to maintain her right to contribute to the creative work of rehearsal.

Words like prima donna get levied against you if you simply have some process that you've come to rely on that works for you. I find there's a greater demand by the director on actresses to abandon themselves to the process that the director wants them to go through. You'll see that same director a half hour later discussing [with a male actor], saying what do you think?

... There was a time when I thought, OK, that's what an actor's supposed to do. You are basically the hand servant of the director. If that director says this is the process that I use, then you're supposed to give over to that and try to do what that director wants.

But then I realized that directors are human beings, too, and they can be as incompetent as the most incompetent actor ... so they have to show you that they have some idea of what they're talking about and that they can get the result that is necessary to make this particular play work.

Now I go into these circumstances much more skeptical. We're all in this together. All of our asses are on the line ... so why should I abandon myself to you when I don't really know who you are or what it is that is going to happen here. So I have something to contribute.

The next stage I went through was that I tried to dazzle them with my ability and that worked for a while. I'd see the director sitting there saying, Oh my God, that's better than anything I thought of. The value of the training I've had [in improvisation] ... is that it's possible for me to come in each day with a completely new slant on a character or to be able to change midstream and say, That's not working? Fine! And without much consideration, switch to a completely different delivery. Most directors find that fascinating. But then I started feeling really strained.... I don't need to prove anything to anybody. My talent is solid. I can do whatever it takes to do the role.

So now the attitude I take most is to assume that I have a right to be a primary contributor.... Until somebody does something to show me that that is not the atmosphere, I proceed in that way. If I have something to say about how something is going in a given scene, I don't look around for permission. I just do it. Then if someone says, I don't want that, I just say, fine.... It's more centered.

I'm not going to walk in with a chip on my shoulder and I'm not going to try to be queen of the world. But I will assume an atmosphere of equality until someone shows me that atmosphere doesn't exist. I just want to make what we're doing the best possible thing that can happen. I'm going to do it with my full energy. I think they find that refreshing because I'm not trying to get over on them or prove anything. I'm just simply saying, I'm here and if I'm not treated in a way that acknowledges that I'm here ... I will say I don't think that I should continue with the project.

I very seldom get to the stage where I have to leave. But if I go to an audition, I consider it an audition for the playwright and the director as well as for myself. I'm there to see if I want to work with them. When I talk to them in that way, they say, wait a minute, who's hiring who here. But if I don't like the way it feels, it's not necessary for me to do it. I'd much rather be a checker in the Safeway than to deal with not being treated as a person in the work that's most important to me.

She acknowledges that not everyone who succeeds artistically and professionally in the theater has the same requirements.

I see [actors and actresses] who can be [self-effacing] and still do good work. They're an absolute blank page and the director can sculpt moment by moment that performance and they'll be brilliant. It used to bother me a lot. I want people to have some inner strength and I see none and yet as performers, they're wonderful. I think that's true of anything. Your ability to come to something doesn't necessarily reflect your inner life.

This description of those performers who can achieve a performance by "taking direction" and doing what they're told seems to beg the question, What is the value of "owning the work"? As one director observes, it is necessary for the performer to believe that he "owns the moment onstage, that he has brought life to it." The performance moment may have been found through a process of interaction with fellow players or the director. It may have been discovered by following leads suggested by someone else in rehearsal. The performer may feel very specific connections to the circumstances or the ideas or the interior life of the play. There may be emotional links with other performers.

Audiences may feel their lives are in some way validated by particular performances. Actors in the New York production of *Glengary Glen Ross* always knew when there were salesmen out front from the enthusiastic interaction of the audience with the play.

When the connections between playwright, director, performers, and audience are established and each of these parties has felt their demands satisfied in some way, then the play works and

Pam Grier and Richard Lawson in *Fool for Love* by Sam Shepard. Photographer: Meridian. Courtesy of the Los Angeles Theatre Center.

becomes an experience that truly transcends the ordinary. The individual benefit that comes out of the collective event for the performer is the knowledge that he has discovered and shaped for himself and for others that extraordinary experience of life. That is the value of "owning the work." I think it is also what keeps people seeking that experience again and again.

Both men and women encounter difficulties with the struggle to "own the work" but this would seem to be one of the areas in theater that is more difficult for women to achieve and maintain. As suggested in the previous chapter, it has to do with developing not a more powerful but an equal voice with men.

The value of "owning the work" is confirmed by a young actress who spent eight years working for carfare in plays in New York before she got her first part in a Broadway production. She says that even if her career does not turn out well, she doesn't think she will ever be bitter about what it has cost her. When she manages to get the job and the performance is good, "the work is so truly your own," she says. "It's one of the great lives you can live."

FIVE

THEY DON'T CALL
IT SHOW ART

In a recent collection of essays, David Mamet describes his understanding of the theater as "the place we go to hear the truth" (Mamet 1986). He is referring to a tradition of theater influenced by Stanislavski, articulated through the Group Theater, the Neighborhood Playhouse, and such teachers as Sanford Meisner, Stella Adler, and Lee Strasberg. The type of training associated with this tradition (and used in many university theater departments) is often called the school of American realism. It enables the performer to live continually in the moment, which is the basis of his or her ability to achieve whatever transformation is called for in the play. A young actor, trained in this tradition and currently struggling with auditions, agents, unions, and rent, says of course he agrees with Mamet's description, "but they call it show business. They don't call it show art." Another actor who has been working in the profession for more than 20 years says, "The stresses between money and art are always there. To try to keep them in proportion ... is hard."

The tension between art and money is often a central fact of life for those who choose to work on the stage. It is a struggle for young performers particularly to do the kind of work that will enable them to grow in their craft and to make more than a hand-to-mouth living. Those in their later years worry about making enough to supplement thin retirement funds when they can no longer remember lines. And actors of all ages, rarely satisfied with where they are in the business, are concerned with the quantity and the quality of the work they may be doing when their present job comes to an end.

The art of theater often grows out of the collaboration of the group. The business of theater requires that every actor must be the agent of his (or her) own success. Many circumstances of the working environment that have to do with the business of theater require self-reliance and blinders-on self-interest. As individuals, performers have to be prepared to make their own opportunities for work. They must develop a process of decision making and shrewd negotiating skills, and cultivate both an aggressive assurance and the fortitude of Job in the face of adversity.

Going into an audition, one actor hears another talk in a businesslike fashion about "selling my goods." Acquiring a sense of oneself as a distinctive commodity (literally referred to in films as "the talent") and developing the entrepreneurial skills to market oneself are not a part of university training. But they have as much to do with getting jobs and furthering one's career as acting ability and training.

Performers not only have to learn their craft, they have to acquire a set of economic survival skills in order to pursue it. Although this may be true for other kinds of artists as well, painters and writers can practice their work without having to depend on being hired to do it. In addition, the circumstances of their daily lives are not determined by how long it takes to get to the theater every night.

The economics of the profession are such that relatively few afford to work only in theater. Even day pay for extras is so much better in films and television that everyone tries to work in as many different forms of entertainment as possible. Members of Screen Actors Guild make $99 to $150 a day as extras (rates effective February 1991 to January 1992). A small scene may bring in $1500 a day, depending on the actor's quote. In contrast, Equity members can make $110, $150 or $210 a week playing a lead working under the small professional theater contract. Mature performers who have made their careers working for adequate salaries in LORT contract theaters often find they could not afford to live on the salaries offered by theaters in Manhattan. When they think of widening their career opportunities, they look for an agent who will get them auditions for film and television projects.

Much more money can be available to performers in film and television. What is not so readily available is challenging material on which to work. Performers point out that, with rare exceptions, films and television are the popular forms of entertainment most eager to please or engage the interest of their viewers. They are least likely to present the audience with the complexity of ideas, emotions, and language that can be found in plays.

To return to Mamet's phrase, I think it may be the tradition of theater as "the place we go to hear the truth," that draws performers back to the stage when they want to measure themselves against that challenge.

Similar Difficulties for Men and Women

Men and women face similar difficulties in struggling with the business part of theater, especially in the critical process of job seeking. A woman director remarks

> In a lot of ways, theater is a very female form of art. Traditionally, women have been more passive. [They] wait to be asked to marry, to date, etc. All actors are like women in that traditional role. They're waiting to be asked, waiting to be picked, ... hoping somebody's going to like them. They're forced to wait to be given the opportunity [to perform]. So there's that frustration. Both men and women feel it.

The frustration described here is part of the nature of the profession. An uncomfortable aspect of the process of job seeking is that it is continual. Both men and women audition, work to convince, and then wait for a casting agent, director, or producer to hire them. When the play or the season or the film or the series is over, the actor's job comes to an end. There may be another job to go to or there may not be. If there is not, then the waiting process begins all over again. A woman director thinks that actors may be better prepared to deal with change because their lives are always in the state of flux.

> [for them] life is constant change. I think actors are very experiential. I started as an actress ... I find great comfort in seeing how things change over time. But it's really getting through change, seeing that you can live through it, that gives you courage to get through the next change.

Speaking from a somewhat different perspective, an actor in his late twenties says, "ultimately you have to fall in love with the uncertainty."

Understanding Oneself as a Commodity

In talking about the effect that his work has had on his life, a young actor describes how his understanding of what gets him acting jobs has grown since he finished his university training.

> It's taught me goal-setting from a business point of view. . . . I was very naive for the first couple of years out of school. I just wanted to be an artist and then I realized that I had this agent negotiating dollars for me. [That] was never taught to me in school. So in that way I have changed. . . . It's made me a lot more aware that I am a commodity.
>
> It's such an intangible thing, talent. This guy's more talented than me so he's going to be making more money? That's a weird thing. You don't have anything on paper like an engineer. He can say, I've a master's degree here and a master's there and a doctorate here. We don't have that.

His physical appearance, his training, and his abilities have fitted him neatly into the category of character man. This has already become a mixed blessing for him. He joined Equity, works regularly, and has already achieved a place in a resident company. However, there is a sameness to the kind of parts he is playing that has begun to bother him. "Because of my character type I rarely get roles that are very far away from me where I have to do a lot of research. I've been pigeonholed into playing [a certain kind of part]. My whole career's been doing that." He has begun to think about losing weight to try to change his physical image in hopes that it will change the way he is presently cast. To him, contract negotiations are the worst part of the business side of working in theater.

> We start out doing this for love and it totally changes. I think in the last four years, I've come into my own as a person and as an artist . . . [I've begun to see] where I fit in this business . . . what kind of commodity I am, the way people see me. I wish they saw me [as] a little more versatile.

An ingenue who was an Equity candidate at 17 agrees that "there's a loss of idealism. I've become more realistic about it. My face is changing and my résumé shots are changing. The more realistic things you have to deal with in theater, the harder it gets."

An actress in her twenties just out of a university program also appears to have an understanding of her assets as a commodity and of how casting people might see her. She, too, has an agent negotiating for her. But she has also had to come to terms with supporting herself with other work when acting jobs are too infrequent to pay the bills.

> I just did a recording. That was the first professional job I had getting out of school, a Shakespeare recording of one scene from *Romeo and Juliet*.... That was great to get because I don't really think of myself [as having a good voice] for recordings. I got a lot of feedback about doing commercials or doing soaps, having a good look for television when I graduated and did the [university] showcase.
>
> During September, I had a situation where I was screentesting for a contract role for [a soap opera] and [her agent] had the whole contract drawn up for three years with all the money outlined. It was a very heady experience.... I know there is an attitude with a lot of actors [that they would not want to do soaps].... But the closer I got to the job, the more I felt that I would feel really good about getting it aside from the money. I was excited about getting the chance of a regular, on-going job.
>
> As far as acting work is concerned, I have come to the point where I have to start being able to support myself when there aren't any acting jobs.

Many roles and therefore more job opportunities are available to the young character man with the ability to play both his age and older. For the actress who is an ingenue, there are opportunities for better money in television but there is also more competition. Both the "character man," in this case a young man who does not look like a hero, and the "ingenue," a pretty young girl, clearly understand and appreciate the value of fitting into those two standard types that are always written into plays. Their agents have no trouble figuring out how to sell them. At the same time, both performers express some uneasiness about the constraints imposed by those stereotypes. It is mind-numbing to think of playing the same type of role over and over again. Although performers value the genre parts that can become their bread and butter, many of them struggle to escape the stereotype. The problem is eventually resolved for women since change is inevitable for the ingenue type when she no longer looks 22. The transition from one age range to another depends on being able to change not only one's own self-image but the preconceived ideas of others. Another actress says, "Even if you see other possibilities for yourself, directors may not."

The problem of casting to type is perhaps worse for those whose physical appearance does not readily fit into any of the conventional casting categories. Young women who would be considered character types may not find that this classification works to their advantage as it often does for men. A wide range of intriguing character roles exists for males in both the older and in recent literature for the theater. The quality and quantity of character roles for women in plays is much more limited, so that character actresses are often hired for one show out of a season. A young character actress remembers, "My first six years of work was touring theaters playing older women who, in real life, would not have been able to afford [to live on] what I worked for or who wanted families." She found that "real age" casting for her meant that she would have to remake herself in the more conventional female image that directors want to see in auditions. Rather than conform to "some whitebread director's prejudice," she began directing, using her own more diverse view of the kinds of people one should see on a stage.

Working in the business has been good for one young actress, she thinks, in that she has learned to set an agenda for herself and find ways to work toward it. "Working professionally, you start having different goals and different values ... those kind of independent goals: where are you going to go and what are you going to do with yourself." She sees a real danger in allowing someone else's appraisal of one's talent and abilities to determine those goals.

> If they're not expecting much from you, you have to have the goal within yourself. If you don't meet it, you can always fall back because they didn't expect much. [but] The more you start looking at what they think of you and not what you think of yourself, that's when you forget what satisfies you.

Working to Support One's Career

I have often thought that restaurants in cities all over the country owe a large debt to the proliferation of theater schools. There is an enormous pool of young, intelligent, well-spoken waiters and waitresses because many of them are only temporarily in the restaurant business. They are really performers working to pay their bills until their next acting job comes along. Food service jobs are convenient for theater people because hours can be negotiated. Days can be kept free for auditions. Food is available. Tips can be good. It is a job that can be picked up and put down easily, according to the vicissitudes in one's career. Its one drawback is that it is usually very hard work. Other kinds of work – telephone sales, word-processing, other types of temporary office work – are less strenuous but may not pay as well.

An actress who has delivered singing telegrams, been a Christmas elf at Macy's ("with a lot of other actors who needed the money"), and worked in a fitness center for performers, and in restaurants, says

> If I have to get a survival job, I like it to be something . . . that's going to leave me feeling that I have a lot left for my acting. . . . Even when you're not acting, you still need to be putting that much energy into being . . . ready to audition, to keep up with classes or working on your voice or your monologues. It's a full-time job whether you've got an acting job or not. . . . You don't want to be doing [something so difficult] that you have no energy left . . . to put into your career, making contacts, and writing letters and keeping your clothes at the dry cleaners so you're ready to go at a moment's notice.

Her concerns about pacing her energy might come from the realization that what she is doing is both psychologically and physically wearing. She mentions the split concentration required in expending energy to keep one job for survival while actively maintaining the career skills for another that is more important to her. Other performers talk about feeling schizophrenic when they have to do this, the sense of marking time, and the fear they have that it is their career that will suffer. This is equally true for performers who maintain nine-to-five positions with more responsibilities and larger salaries and benefits. A Black actress with such a job in Manhattan talks about her decision to leave the security of that position to work full-time in the theater.

> I've been getting good response from agents on [her last show] and they're going to start sending me out I hope. That's the practical consideration. The other is even more important and more personal and that is, I need to act. . . . That's what actors in New York contend with all the time. The dichotomy is, I have a nice job. It is a good job. It pays me good money [but] I have this other life.
> The nature of the beast for many actors here is [that they are] living schizophrenic lives.

Performers who work in the many good smaller companies in other cities will find these comments very familiar. Pay scales in these theaters, although they may be improving, still require that performers support themselves with other jobs as well.

Working at "civilian" jobs also provides a way to finance the continual expenses that accrue in actively looking for work in theater. Auditions arranged by a manager at one end of the country or the other entail travel expenses that may not be reimbursed. Taxis, phone calls, food, and clothes all tend to be more expensive in major urban centers. Making investments in travel, expenses, and upkeep reinforces the performers' image of themselves as a commodity. Although these are legitimate business expenses that are an unavoidable part of the profession, it is discouraging on a very personal level to have the investment not pay off in the form of a job.

With these problems in mind, an actor of some years ago left a bequest in his will for what has become known as the "shoe fund." This is a fund administered through Equity where members who are out of work can present their union card and receive a voucher for a pair of free shoes from designated stores in New York. The bequest must have been either quite substantial or carefully managed since I know of two generations of performers who have gotten shoes from it.

Dealing with the Business as Equals

Learning to protect oneself in negotiations with management is a problem for men and women, especially the beginning performer. A young actor describes his first Equity job at a summer stock house in New England. After he signed a contract for $400 a week, the producer privately proposed to pay him $40 a week and the promise of a job every summer after that. When other Equity members heard about the deal, they reported it to the union and that ended the summer for all of them.

> Apparently, he owned three stock theaters and had fifteen people, five at each theater, under this deal, who had been intimidated to go along with it.... Equity said, "You've got to pay these people." He said, "I don't have the money." They closed down all the theaters. They went into a year of arbitration and we got all our back salary.

Unfortunately, every union–versus–unscrupulous management story doesn't necessarily end with actors getting their money. A group of new Equity members went to work for an Equity theater in a Southern state where the producer had been allowed to pay only part of his bond. The bond covers two weeks' salary and travel pay for Equity performers and was instituted in the early days of the union to prevent exactly what happened in this case. When the producer did not pay performers' contracted salaries, the union instructed the company to return to New York. After they got there, expecting their salaries plus travel expenses, it was discovered that the full bond had not been posted and no one got any money. Since arbitration in such cases can be lengthy, an actor who was involved says he still stops by the Equity office occasionally to see if there has been a settlement.

An actress from the company remembers going home and pouring over the union rule book after the show at night: "It was our second or third Equity job.... We're studying the book every night because he could tell us anything. What do we know? ... And he knew that, the producer."

An actress discusses the dilemma of finding that the requirements of the business can be used against what is perhaps one of the major tools the actor works with, his vulnerability.

> I think there's something intrinsic to working in the theater that has to do with being childlike. That's a quality that can occupy a secret place in one's soul. That's something that can be there or not be there, but it's ageless.
>
> But the assumption from the theatrical environment is that that ageless quality means that you are "as a child" and should be treated as a child. That's very difficult to accept as one comes into one's maturity. It's very easy for producers, directors, agents, theatrical administrators to exercise their power over actors in a way that attempts to create adult-child relationships.
>
> Maturity for me implies something solid, genuine as opposed to the trappings; and when you have that solid core, then none of that [treatment] makes sense anymore. When you begin to want to take the reins of your life in your own hands and deal as business equals, the "business" doesn't want you to do that.

There are other difficulties that come with the realization of maturity. An actress talks about how much more difficult it becomes to risk oneself in front of people who may know nothing about how actors work and with whom there is no relationship of trust.

It becomes harder to audition. It's harder to put yourself in that position.... When you're young, you have an audacious energy and you don't really care. The older you get, the more sensitive you get as a person and it becomes more difficult to put yourself in a humiliating situation. It gets harder to warm up. There's a part of you who thinks that getting up in front of people is silly. It's a children's game. The older you get, the more clearly you see that.

In realizing these things, I've examined my commitment to it and found I can't not do it. It's the way I contact the world. I focus my view through acting. The best theater causes people to respond, to feel things, to be educated, to have a real insight. There are things that are wrong with my profession. But there are things that are good, too, positive, life-enforcing, inspirational. Theater has been a real instrument of growth for me. It gives me focus.

Union rules offer some protection to performers but beyond certain basic contract agreements, they also take time and energy to work out. An actor who has spent 15 years in a resident company talks about the frustration he feels when problems arise at the theater which have nothing to do with the artistic work. He has often found that he resents

the time and concentration it takes on a problem, especially if you're Equity deputy. It's not so much that the management is out to screw the actor. But it's the same ugly problem. It's solved and then goes underground. Five years later, it reappears. And you think, wait a minute! Didn't we have some understanding on this? It's not malicious. The stresses between money and art are always there. To try to keep them in proportion and to diffuse them is hard.

The business can also present opportunities for what most people would consider unreasonable personal danger. One actress who works in films frequently describes a difficult experience having to do with an improperly set-up stunt in a low-budget film. In a complicated driving sequence at night on an icy road, she was asked to simulate the turning of the steering wheel because the production company did not want to spend the time or the money to unhook the steering column of the car. The car was attached to and controlled by a tow truck on which the camera was mounted.

It was a nightmare. It was impossible for me to figure out that the car was turning. Then I'm supposed to act and smoke and deliver my lines. I kept saying this is not going to work.... I had to do a similar stunt after working all night and after one of my hardest scenes. Then we went back to this tow rig to do another piece. It was three in the morning and the director yelled, turn! So I turned. The truck went one way and the car went the other. Fortunately, no one was hurt.

The experience taught her to be more critical of the people she works with and she has since turned down a job when the staff for the project did not seem competent. Several people who work in films, both men and women, describe similar episodes in which they were asked to do action sequences that ordinarily would require trained stunt people. An actor describes how he worked at the driving sequence he had agreed to, focusing on the specifics of the task to keep himself calm and in control of the scene. He also speaks to the question of what actors learn to do with their feelings of powerlessness, particularly on film sets.

> I did the best thing I could in the situation. I didn't drive any faster than I could handle the car no matter what they said.
>   It was not my mistake. Actors tend to blame themselves first and it's usually not their fault. The problem is usually from outside. Often you end up being put in a situation of danger where your only alternative to doing the work is to make a scene that could affect your future possibilities.

Like films, commercials done for a local market such as the Baltimore-Washington area are a major source of income for performers but auditions for them can be soul-destroying events. An older actress has learned to view the ordeal of trying to please the product sponsor, the ad agency, the production company, and the casting people as just another performance. "It makes your whole outlook different if you go there with a sense of competence. You just do the best you can. It doesn't mean anything unless you fit the concept they have and there's no way to get around that."

National commercials are done on a somewhat grander scale with full production units, mobile dressing rooms, and caterers. Initial fees and residuals from nationally shown commercials are viewed as gold mines by performers. They take only a day or two and can fund the actor through any number of slow months when even the auditions run out. But national commercials are not easy to get. One young actor estimates from his own and his friends' experience that "getting one out of every thirty you read for is a good average."

Another actor bemoans the money he spent on a class in

auditioning for commercials. The positive affirmation technique that was taught worked for others in the class but he could never do his "affirmations" without making them into comedy routines. He describes a particular group of performers who only do commercials. "They do not take theater or film jobs at all because they don't want to leave the city, New York or LA, where they make their [enormous amounts] of money, for fear of missing auditions. But they still call themselves actors." After listening to a group of young people discuss their audition classes, an older actor says,

> It's like the cargo cults in the Pacific after the War. You don't know what got you the last job but you know that you need to feel that you have some control over the situation. So you invent all kinds of rules and rituals that may be meaningless but if they give you some measure of confidence, you think they're going to help.

He is convinced that performers must learn careful habits in managing money so that the jobs that pay well can carry them through leaner times. The days when he lived on peanut butter and rye bread have made him skeptical of extravagant living unless it is part of his per diem. The rationale he makes for his business investments is that they must be conservative since he works in a high risk profession. When he hears of an actor who had had great success and then in less than ten months, lost a house, a Jaguar, and a Mercedes, he says

> It's not an uncommon story but any actor who has managed to make enough money to buy all of those things only to lose them ten months later hasn't learned one of the actor's most basic survival skills: how to manage the money you do make at whatever level.

Power Relationships and the Status of the Actor

Not much is written about the generosity with which performers subsidize live theater, working for less because they want to be working. Not many professions pay so undependable a return on four to six years of training. But this spirit of generosity can easily be exploited by other parts of the business. One reason for referring again to playwright David Mamet is that he has given some thought to the underlying reasons for the performer's disadvantaged position. In *Writing in Restaurants*, Mamet describes a hierarchy of power represented by director, producer and relative performer.

Gail Grate as Eliza Doolittle with Terrence Currier and Richard Bauer as Professor Higgins in Shaw's *Pygmalion*. Photographer: Joan Marcus. Courtesy of Arena Stage.

> Those who come in last, who come in at the bottom – the actors – are subject to the unreasoned, unloving, and frightened whims of those in [financial] power over them.... This unreasoned commercial hierarchy of actor-director-producer has drained the theater of its most powerful force: the phenomenal strength and generosity of the actor; and, as in any situation of unhappy tyranny, the oppressed must free the oppressor [Mamet 1986, 32-33].

The solution to the problem which Mamet suggests is one that performers learn to use in a variety of ways. A number of performers interviewed, both men and women, have dealt with the sense of powerlessness by redefining theater in their own terms and creating their own work. In some cases, this involves actually founding a new theater. Fourteen of the 50 people interviewed here have established theaters or programs to address issues and audiences that they felt were being neglected. Fourteen have developed and successfully marketed community education programs and acting workshops. Fifteen have assumed all or part of the day-to-day administration of existing theaters. Six others hold or have held major positions with theater support groups.

It's possible that as the commercial theater in New York continues to shrink, and the shape of theater continues to change in this country, performers will find new opportunities for a more equitable share in the power structures of theater. One of the ways in which that might be accomplished could be through more effective use of the actor's union. As art and money are often at odds in the theater, the actor's self-reliance and his investment in the group are equally at odds over the union.

Actors on Actors' Equity Association

Whatever problems performers may have with Equity, complaints are usually prefaced by expressions of appreciation for adequate salary scale, contract agreements on working conditions, hours, and other benefits and protections that did not exist for performers before the advent of the union. Rehearsal and travel pay, limits on hours worked, adequate backstage facilities, a mechanism for negotiation with management—all became standard conditions for working performers only after the formation of the union.

An actor who has had his problems with Equity still affirms a larger value in the achievements of working people who fought for and won economic advantages and protections using effective political tools provided by union organization.

> It goes beyond any individual needs. I look at it on a class basis. It is to protect the rights of people.... Certainly, Equity does protect actors in benefits, conditions, better salaries.... I think that the unions do protect not only those who belong to [them] but everybody else. I have social security, unemployment insurance, all those [protections] that we have today because working people fought for them, not because [somebody] gave them to us on a plate.

After that has been said, however, many actors also feel that as a group they suffer from too many unions. Most of them belong to at least three, AEA (Actors' Equity Association), SAG (Screen Actors Guild), and AFTRA (American Federation of Television and

Radio Artists). Each union requires its own set of dues, maintains its own governing body, and provides its own set of health and welfare benefits, which in theory should all be available to the individual union member. In practice, it is difficult enough to arrange the paperwork to get any one union to cover health costs and nearly impossible to lay claim successfully to all three plans even though the performer may be eligible to do so. Since Equity is the poor sister of the three, its health benefits are the least comprehensive and the least generous.

An actor points out that all the union health plans have been strained by the rapid spread of the AIDS virus.

> They've been sapped of all their money. It's hit the union health plans so hard. Something they never predicted that has affected everyone else. For instance, when I have a back problem, I can only go to the chiropractor 12 times a year. Eighty percent is covered but ... to get your back adjusted, it takes ten visits and there's your whole year's quota. If it happens again later on in the year, you're screwed.

Equity's health plan has been so depleted in recent years that the union has had to restructure the terms of members' eligibility along the lines of the SAG and AFTRA plans. All members must have worked 12 weeks or earned a minimum of $5000 under any Equity contract to qualify for a year's coverage. Work records are reviewed and updated every three months. Under the new terms, although the pool of those covered (without self-pay) is diminished, coverage is increased for those who are working.

Other Changes in the Union

"Years ago if you started working onstage in Washington," an actor tells me, "the most common piece of advice about getting your Equity card was that the union should send it with a ticket to New York stapled to the back." The union expected actors to come to New York to get jobs even when much of the work was out of town. When performers complained about that situation, a union spokesman reminded them that coal miners weren't doing well in New York City either.

Those attitudes have changed somewhat for both performers and the union. But beginning performers are still advised by those already in the profession not to join the union until they can clearly see that it is to their advantage. At the unemployment office in Jersey City, a young actor has difficulty explaining to his counselor that although his union is associated with the AFL-CIO, it assumes no obligation to get him a job and has no local representative whom he can contact.

Even young performers working in New York are beginning to complain of rules that appear to "give away" the advantage of union membership. Among these advantages were the open call auditions, available only to union members. These auditions provided opportunities to performers working without an agent to arrange auditions for them. In effect, the union arranged auditions, negotiating with producers to ensure that Equity members would have a chance to be considered for parts. That rule has now been changed to allow nonunion performers at these auditions. As a result, the auditions have become so crowded that union members are discouraged from coming to them. An Equity actress explains, "If you've worked in [an Equity] show, [but are] not an Equity member, it makes you eligible for Equity auditions, which makes open calls almost impossible now. There really is no reason to join Equity if they have this policy."

She also complains about the union's rulings over the past ten years that have often had the unintended effect of making it cheaper for producers to use performers to whom they had formerly paid union scale. "A nonunion actor working in a nonunion theater can be making $250 a week. I was working in a small professional theater company and making [less]. For people who are not members of the union, it's great."

The small professional theater contract which allows theaters of a certain size to hire Equity actors for less than minimum salaries set by the union may be an attempt on the part of the union to acknowledge and respond to the shrinking of the commercial theater and the development of many different levels of theater in New York and throughout the country over the past 40 or more years.

"It was created because people were being prevented from working in good non–Equity theaters and there were a lot of complaints," a performer says, explaining her understanding of how this contract came about. "People were saying, not only do you not find us work but you prevent us from getting work in places that are reputable if we choose to work for less."

Working under any Equity contract provides professional standards of protection in the work place. This is a real advantage to performers in dealing with theater managements whose level of experience and access to resources vary so widely. An actress says, "They can't keep you [at rehearsal] until two in the morning. They have to give you regular breaks." But if controlling the budget deficit is a pervasive problem for midsize resident theaters, cash flow is often critical for smaller theaters. An actor remembers accepting an expensive suit from the costume shop when salary money ran out at a theater where he worked under the SPT (i.e., "small professional theater") contract. So there is a question about whether Equity actors benefit economically from the small professional theater contract. Under it, they have more opportunities to work. However, older actors question whether one can be said to be working in the profession if one is not being paid enough to live on without a supplementary income, or being paid in suits.

As late as the 1960s, no professional performer would have used the phrase "good non–Equity theaters." The line was sharply drawn between Equity theaters that employed union actors and community "little" theaters where people enjoyed doing plays as a hobby. As in the 1960s theaters were formed in many areas of the country outside of New York with artistic goals, administrative structures, and circumstances of production that differed significantly from Broadway, so in the 1970s and 1980s other levels of theater have come into existence that differ from major regional theaters. With seating capacities ranging from 99 to 200 or 300, these smaller theaters present audiences with the opportunity to experience many kinds of theater at a more intense level. They offer new opportunities to minority performers and playwrights and develop new audiences for works that would probably not be done in more conventional venues. They make theater available to those who could not afford more expensive entertainment. That many of these small theaters are started by performers, directors, and playwrights with professional training and professional credentials but without the money to pay union salaries further blurs the line between professional and nonprofessional theater in a way that is relatively new.

The actor's union has been slow to recognize how changes in regional theater and the levels of smaller theater that have developed in recent years have affected the lives of actors and actresses who work in them. The union's mechanism for monitoring and controlling new levels of theater has been the introduction of special contracts, designed to apply to specific types of theater, ranging from Broadway to regional to dinner theater to waiver theater in Los Angeles. Seating capacity is one of the distinguishing features that categorizes type.

In the 1950s when the first League of Regional Theater contracts were worked out, no one knew how this different way of doing theater would affect the lives of performers. Union operations were centralized in New York and union performers in regional theaters spread across the country had little time or opportunity to assume an active role in setting union policy. An actress asks impatiently how actors who rehearse one show while playing another for ten months a year with one day off a week can ever make themselves heard by their union which may be at the other end of the country. "I don't know if our representation will ever be [adequate]. How can it be? We're here all the time." As someone who has been working in regional theater for 20 years, her experience has been that the union collected her dues but did not keep her very well informed. She says, "I lived [and worked at a regional theater] for ten years before I received one postcard announcing an Equity meeting. I would have gone to Equity meetings had I known they existed. How is it I didn't know?"

One of a sizeable number of performers who have spent their careers in regional theater, she recognizes that when these kinds of theaters began, they employed actors on a six-week contract. Perhaps because of that, much of the union's frame of reference for regional theater is still based on the short-term contract. However, one of the first Ford Foundation grants to Arena Stage in the 1960s was made to establish a salary of $200 a week for performers to encourage the formation of a company of actors who would perform together for a ten-month season. The idea of building acting companies at resident theaters began to provide professional actors and actresses with the possibility of a different quality of life from that period. The status provided by a salary guaranteed by the Ford Foundation could enable an actor to buy a house, afford a family, acquire a perception of self as part of an on-going community larger than the current production.

In the years since that first Ford grant, regional theaters still hire performers for six weeks but they also hire people for a full season. If the arrangement works for both theater and performer, contracts can lengthen to several years or ten years. When a group works particularly well together, the audience, the performers, the work they do, and the theater itself realize benefits in the quality of the work achieved. It is not uncommon to find performers who have learned their craft at several theaters across the country or at one theater where they may have worked for 10 to 20 years.

In 1960, that Ford Foundation salary of $200 a week exceeded the Equity minimum salary at the time. Whether or not a precedent was set by that grant, regional theater salaries have generally been above minimums set by the union. Likewise, union regulations that set a standard for the physical work environment are not often a point of contention in LORT theaters since most were built or remodelled to conform to those conditions.

What are the requirements that performers in regional theaters cite as being specific to the needs of their work? Since, in many instances, they are working at two shows at the same time (rehearsing one show during the day and performing another at night), performers need specific rules to help them conserve their time and energy.

When asked about the number of hours he spends at the theater when doing a heavy role, an actor says, "Normally more than seventy-two hours a week. . . . Fifty-two is what the theater is supposed to get." An actress who has worked in resident companies agrees the hours are long and questions the demands that can be made on those who work this hard over a long period of time. "One day off a week. It's archaic. It's designed for the old view of actors as gypsies, with no real lives."

After years of this work load, actors can begin to feel exhausted and claustrophobic. An actress accustomed to doing heavy roles talks about the order of priorities in rehearsal.

> I did *Hedda Gabler,* a tremendous line-load. The opening was in three weeks and my costume fittings were in the hour break that we took. I had to work the overtime. I would have paid five times that much to get them to leave me alone and let me have a nap.

An actress suggests that tax advisors who would be available locally would be a great help. Whether they are self-employed or on salary, performers have always had complicated tax situations. This has not improved with recent changes in the law. The union does provide assistance but members must go to New York to get it and appointments may not be scheduled in advance. "Imagine if you're [working] in Des Moines," someone says.

Making a critical assessment of the union's relation to its members who work in regional theater, a director who works in that area as well says

> The Equity system now tends to make the life of a resident actor
> too close to the life of an itinerant performer and expects [the per-
> former to have] the same kind of detachment from the producing
> organization that the itinerant performer needs to have to survive.

He cites the necessity of touring performers to negotiate salary,
transportation, conditions in the workplace, and other protections
on a job to job basis. Performers who move from theater to theater
need union standards set because the "standards vary so widely in
terms of conditions of the work place and the attitudes of producers.
An itinerant actor works under a number of kinds of contracts
whereas a resident actor works under one contract. The multiplicity
of contracts is a benefit to the itinerant because he is protected no
matter where he goes."

For some actors or for actors in some period in their lives, this
will always be true. The many different kinds of union contracts will
always provide the protective regulations that union members can
use to assure them adequate conditions of work. However, he also
points out that

> When conditions are unique as in a resident theater, the resident
> contract doesn't address the needs of the resident actor ... mostly
> in the area of lifestyle not so much in the area of finance ... hours
> worked, hours spent in the theater, attention being paid to the
> acknowledgment of a family life or a religious life.

Only in the past ten years has the union negotiated to rearrange
performances and rehearsals so that no rehearsals are called and no
performances are scheduled on Thanksgiving, Christmas Eve or
Christmas Day.

Actors with families, particularly where there are teenage
children, often stretch themselves between the energies concentrated to resolve problems at home and the energies that must be
focused on performance. Even if there are no family responsibilities
that need to be addressed, the creative energy that performers use
in their work eventually wears thin unless they are allowed quiet
periods. Someone compares the feeling of being emotionally drained
and out of ideas to sleep experiments where the patient is awakened
on a certain schedule and asked to recount their dreams. But the
schedule is too abrupt to allow the patient to reach the period of sleep
when dreams occur. So there are no dreams to describe.

An actor who has served on a local liaison committee for Equity suggests that the chief difficulty with union organization is that it is still too centralized. He finds ironic parallels between the problems that many performers have in dealing with their union and the difficulties that Russians face in trying to reshape the centralization of their bureaucracy.

> If they relinquished some of the control out of New York, they would find the returns a lot better. . . . They try to do so much with so little. They use the different contracts to keep control over this whole animal [the theater], and they think they're monitoring the contracts. But they can't monitor the LORT contracts, for example. Regional theater is everywhere but New York. . . .
> They need to put autonomous branches out to the locals so that people can get more involved. . . . They would have a lot better success in organizing and in many other things if they did that.

He notes that, in contrast to Equity, the American Federation of Television and Radio Artists and the Screen Actors Guild maintain local offices in many areas and he lists the benefits of that system.

> The local here deals with our affairs. We have our own budget. We keep our own money. . . . I find that much better . . . people get more involved. They have a vested interest, not only in terms of money but in terms of their energy. They have a body they can call up on the local telephone when they have a problem. That's the difference. Equity is less known, less understood by the general public than AFTRA or SAG. People are clamoring to belong to AFTRA and SAG. Nobody is clamoring to belong to Equity.

When Equity was founded, a performer points out, theater was a major business where enormous amounts of money could be made. Today, films and television as the purveyors of American entertainment are among those industries that dominate the international business world. Live theater has its place but fortunes are rarely made there.

An actress associates the relative status of the union with the bargaining position of those in the profession. "It's a extremely weak union. When the unemployment rate is so high among actors, we can't negotiate our position." At the same time, she adds that the experience of being part of a resident company provides "a more stable environment. As a collection of people we are more and more conscious of not disenfranchising ourselves. . . . And hopefully, because of that, we'll be able to make better use of the union."

Like the actor who said he sees the value of the union in larger terms than his individual needs, these last comments point up an understanding of the union as a political entity that will only be as effective as its members can make it. The positive value of the union is understood to be not in its bureaucracy of committees and councils but in the achievements of people who struggle collectively to improve their position.

The Union as a Voice for Minority Performers

For most performers, there is a tension between individual interest and recognition of power in the group. In a profession where intense competition requires that individuals must learn to aggressively protect their own interest, many people also know from the experience of their working lives the powerful force that can be wielded by a group working together for a common purpose. At the same time, theater people take most seriously the idea that "the respect is in the work." The extraordinary performance or achievement is highly valued, and assumes an importance that overshadows other considerations.

All of these elements seem to have contributed to the controversy over nontraditional casting in the case of *Miss Saigon*. When Equity first recognized the complaint of an Asian-American playwright and an actor, a cynical observer predicted that the show would eventually come in with the white actor in the lead with a $50 million advance sale instead of $25 million because of the extra publicity. The appropriateness of the union's decision seemed questionable to begin with since the white actor in this case had been defined as a star. This category is usually considered outside the rules regulating casting quotas. The economic advantage of a star performer to an incoming Broadway show is generally recognized by union and management.

Agents representing the white actor circulated petitions and collected enough signatures from union performers to require Equity to reexamine and finally reverse its decision. Public statements from other members of Equity supported reversing the union's decision and often cited the extraordinary performance of the actor in question as the chief argument in favor of that action. Articles appeared in the *New York Times* describing the tradition in films of using recognizable stars in major roles rather than performers of the ethnic groups called for in the script. These articles seemed to be an attempt to educate the general reader on the meager opportunities afforded American performers with Asian heritage in films or in that part of the theater where salaries are substantial.

There were few public statements by Asian-American performers. Whether those members of the union were surprised by initial lack of support in public statements from other members of Equity, considered it a poor test case, or could not find many opportunities to make their views known, no strong voice emerged to argue the minority position. One of the artists who did respond, spoke to a number of complex issues involved. An Amerasian playwright quoted in the *Los Angeles Times,* supported the right of the minority Equity members to bring their complaint to the union. But she thought that the injustice suffered by minority performers would not be lessened by preventing another actor's performance. She pointed out what most of the public discussion ignored: that the character in question is described in the script as biracial, which has its own complex pschology, neither Anglo nor Asian. Her understanding of nontraditional casting supported by the union is that "the majority of roles go to white male artists . . . [and] the policy of nontraditional casting was created . . . to [increase] professional opportunities that would combat the historical prejudice." She reaffirms her commitment to this policy. At the same time, she argues that

> Minority artists must choose their battles carefully. If a battle is fought with blurred vision, the cause is set back. The "Saigon" role was not the best battleground because it is a complex issue. . . . The crimes are: misunderstanding race (an American affliction), the legacy of racism in the American theater, and the manipulation of the true spirit of non-traditional casting. Keeping Pryce [the white actor] from performing is not going to solve these crimes or appease the victims [Houston 1990, F3].

The real value in continuing to talk about nontraditional casting in theater events like *Miss Saigon* would seem to be that the arguments for minority performers can be carried beyond the circle of wagons formed by the conservative theater establishment. Newspaper accounts described at some length the limited opportunities for minority actors. Readers could see that minority pressure for equal opportunity has made real progress in the business world and the professions but relatively little in some areas of theater. One effect of the *Saigon* controversy has already been an inquiry into hiring practices in theater by the New York City Commission on Human Rights. Another is that the AFL-CIO has begun to express interest in better job opportunities for minority performers. Perhaps the wider forum for discussion has provided the impetus for Asian-American performers in New York and in Los Angeles to demand a stronger voice for their concerns within the union.

The Invalid Theater and Two Rich Relatives

Every ten years or so, critics predict the death of live theater in the United States. Production costs are prohibitive. Broadway remains a theatrical archetype for both audiences and performers but new American plays are rarely produced there anymore. Musical spectacles that emphasize stage technology have become much more lucrative investments for producers. And those who can afford the tickets want mainly to be entertained.

Certainly, there are fewer Broadway theaters in use today than there were in 1950. However, many more levels of theater exist both in New York and throughout the country. For whatever reasons, live theater has not only survived but proliferated in unexpected ways and unlikely circumstances.

It is the place where performers learn their craft. There is no preparation or training for the other media without it. A Black stage actor, enjoying the luxury of two hit films in the past year says, "No one can teach you to act. You learn ... in front of an audience." Theater provides the training ground where such skills as script analysis, character development, concentration, focus, language, timing must prove out for the performer in terms of what does or does not work in front of an audience. Increasingly, live theater develops the talent pool that films and television draw from. Two performers argue that those more lucrative branches of the entertainment business might find a way to "pay back" live theater for its role in the training and development of talent. But that does not seem very likely in the tight money atmosphere of the 1990s.

In the meantime, there are surely easier ways to gratify one's ego and make a living. Perhaps it is a heady experience to be able to explore some significant truth and then have the opportunity to represent that aspect of reality to other people. Those performers who spend most of their lives working on stage pay for the sense of power it gives them in fewer material benefits and limited public recognition. Theater in this country is subsidized by actors who will work for less than they should because they have a passion for what they do. For some, that passion is bolstered by the conviction that the humanizing experience shared between playwright, director, actors, and audience will ultimately benefit the larger society.

SIX

MAKING A LIFE
OUTSIDE THE THEATER

One of the genuine gifts of my life is that I have married an actor who is also an avid hobbyist. I know that he has taken up another one when books, tools, instruction sheets or pieces of special clothing begin to pile up under the bed, on the kitchen table, or wherever he is. A partial list of his projects over 30 years includes refinishing furniture, stamp and coin collecting, opera, making dandelion wine, power saws, power walking, sailing, bird and bug watching, photography, flying, golf, fishing, casting fortunes in lead on New Year's Eve, building bookcases, old house renovation, stocks and bonds, origami, dog- and attempted-cat training, spread-sheet construction, raising tropical fish, brick-laying, making catsup, tree box horticulture, original embroidery on denim shirts, picture framing, aerobic bicycling, and country music.

Hobbies have been a great help to Bob in getting him through some years when he played whatever roles he got, not because they interested him but because he had bills to pay and a family to feed. In one particularly barren season, he began to hang around the small scruffy airfields close to the city. For Christmas that year I gave him a certificate for flying lessons at one of them. He came home from the first and decided he needed a short jacket and scarf. He passed the written test, did solos, and started cross country flights, collecting hours in the air and working his way towards a license. Then he began to get bigger parts and no longer had the time to keep up his hours. He also admitted that he was a little relieved to give it up. He had never made a landing by himself without howling at the top of his lungs with fear. For a while, flying had given him the sense of risk and exhilaration he felt when he really enjoyed working on stage.

Most performers have similar periods of frustration in their careers. Those who can find some way of using outside interests to get away from their problems spare themselves and those around them a good deal of grief.

When I asked another actor in the course of an interview about his life outside the theater, he said, "A life outside the theater? I'm not sure that I have one. I think I'm still waiting for that to begin." For some actors, his answer might describe a state of mind, I think, rather than a literal situation. When I asked the question, I had in mind not only the kinds of projects that performers often take up to stop drumming on the furniture and worrying about their work, but also the various networks of family, friends, neighbors, business associates, and acquaintances with whom some common interest has been shared.

Performers I know have developed interests in competitive running, making gospel music, coaching soft ball teams, working with Alzheimer's patients, obliterating world hunger, collecting antique weather vanes, and raising German shepherds. The man I was talking with had many friends and interests but the circle of people he was completely comfortable with were people he knew in the theater. He had spent a number of years working in one place and although he had made connections with groups of "civilians," he saw himself outside their world. He felt somewhat nervous about what those people thought of him, whereas he was completely confident and "at home" in his work.

This may be a hazard of any occupation in which one becomes totally absorbed but I think it has particular resonance for theater people. Because of the concentration and the hours that are required, performers conciously or unconsciously isolate themselves from everything except the work. They appear to put their real lives to one side for a time. Picking up the threads again is easier for some people than it is for others. The day after the closing of a difficult show, an actor describes "walking around with unfinished sentences, not having a sense of purpose." An actress says "It's such a regimented schedule when you're doing a play with seven or eight shows a week ... when that whole world that has been created that you enter night after night suddenly stops, you find yourself a little at a loss." The feelings described here are temporary but they may contribute to any larger sense of isolation that an individual might have.

Living in any kind of family situation provides some insurance against that sense of isolation. Real life problems that have to be solved make an effective connection to the rest of the world. Ties of affection that need to be tended if they are to continue to grow provide continuity and a larger sense of purpose to one's life. This seems to work better for women who are accustomed to using family and friends as a regular activity in their lives. Like many women who work, actresses apparently assume most of the household management as well as their work outside the home. That conditions of work are often temporary and actual job sites change, can be both an asset and a liability in making these arrangements.

Most of the World Works from Nine to Five

Most of the world works from nine to five with weekends off. Vacation time, sick leave, and holiday time can be efficiently consolidated around long weekends. Performers expect their work to occupy a much larger proportion of their time when they are working. And when they are not working, invariably they are worrying about when they will be working again.

Television and film work often begins at five in the morning and may continue at various levels of overtime until the shooting schedule is over for the day. This time may be spent working or it may be spent waiting around to work, depending on the size of the role and how the particular project is organized. Performers must be told they have been released for the day before they can go home. Sundays are normally free (except when special locations can only be used on that day) but Saturdays may be work days on location. Films are shot on either a five or a six day work schedule. Free days don't necessarily fall on weekends. The shooting schedule determines holiday time. A thriving television series may take a hiatus (vacation) from April to July. For a less successful series, fewer shows may be ordered and filming may be over by December.

In the theater, rehearsals begin in the late morning or at noon and run to four or five if there is a show that night. If there is no show, rehearsals may continue after a dinner break or the evening may be devoted to note sessions with the director. Technical rehearsals where production details are worked out and runthroughs followed by director's notes make special demands on time and energy. Longer plays are especially difficult on matinee days. Equity requires that union members be given one day off each week, usually Monday. Since holidays often draw the biggest audiences, they tend to be work days for theater people. Thanksgiving and Christmas are recent exceptions. Within the last ten years, theater managements have begun to give Thanksgiving Day, Christmas Eve, and Christmas Day off, using the regular dark days when there are no scheduled shows to make up rehearsal time and performances.

When my own sons were children, we planned Thanksgiving dinner around the theater schedule and went to see their father in whatever show he was doing on Christmas night. The reason we lived within 15 minutes of the theater was so that Bob could come home for dinner and talk to his children once a day while they were growing up.

Added to the unique daily routine of performers' lives is the possibility of each new job being in a different part of the country or the world. For many people this is exhilarating but it can also interupt close relationships. Perhaps as a consequence, performers look for a sense of community in those they work with that they may not always find. When they do find it, they also know that community will dissolve when the project is over. A young actress describes the difficulty she has with this aspect of the profession.

> You're making a real connection with a human being as opposed to taking for granted who that person is. It's when the whole thing ends and you lose these real lives that you've made connections to — that feels very transient, and it's not helpful to your real life. It's as if you have a whole other family and when the show closes, you do feel like you've lost a part of yourself. Then the next show comes along and you have a new family. That's the part of the theater that is painful. It's like a small, small death.

This might be more of a problem for people at the beginning of their careers. The longer one works, the better one's chances of finding former friends or colleagues in the same company. An actress who has spent a very long life in the theater maintains her many friendships by carrying on an extensive personal correspondence. Letters are a regular part of her daily schedule and her correspondents include both friends who work in theater and former next-door neighbors.

Patterns of Friendship

Performers spend so much time together in the theater that extraordinary support systems can develop between them. Support
may consist of lending money, suggesting someone for a role,
trading childcare, sharing an apartment, or working patiently with
those who have mental problems or difficulties with alcoholism. Many
performers recognize that friendships in theater may not be based
on the same rules or follow the same pattern as friendships outside
theater. A stage manager says

> Relationships develop in the theater that have the ability to be
> lopped off at the head when a parting takes place and seem to be
> able to pick up again right where they left off and then can stand
> another lopping and another picking up. Reasonably close relation-
> ships can survive that way in the theater in a way that's very
> different from the way other people experience friendship.

Performers also share an understanding of the energy levels required for performance. What may seem like selfishness, disinterest
or narcissism to outsiders, performers understand as a mechanism
for gathering one's resources for the work that has to be done. A
young actress says

> No one keeps me out of my house, especially before show. Gotta
> have that time before the show to do nothing. Nothing! I start get-
> ting nervous when I see four o'clock coming. [I say] OK, gotta go,
> gotta run now. Can't talk to you. Not that I go home and do anything
> in particular but I feel that if I take that time for myself, I'll be really
> focused on every show.

People who do not work in the profession do not always understand the necessity for quiet or the residual effects that a role may
have for a performer. A film actress talks about this problem in
relationships.

> It used to be hard for me to know that people who worked around
> actors all the time didn't understand that when we were cold, it was
> not directed at anyone. It was something that had to be done so we
> could do the work. Now I've accepted that people don't understand.
>   On one track in my mind, that character is always there, always
> present. When you're working on something, you're there whether
> you're actually filming or not. At least I am. I can't be totally

> detached. . . . Work always spills over into life. Some people don't
> understand that. They feel very threatened. They don't know who's
> going to be there for breakfast.

Different hours, different attitudes toward work experience, a
different expectation and experience of change, different patterns
of friendship, a different level of involvement in one's interior resources – all of these separate performers from those who do
something else for a living. In continual jobseeking, performers
become skillful in emphasizing those aspects of personality that
might be most attractive to potential employers. Eventually, this
can become a facade or public persona which is then a useful shield
for the private person in public situations.

The Value of a Public Persona

There are performers who have difficulty, outside of the
framework of a play or film, getting up in front of a group as just
themselves, to accept an award or make a speech. These are competent actors who are never uncomfortable on stage or in front of a
camera. They describe themselves and other performers like them
as being shy. This appears to be more often true of stage performers
than people who work in films and television although there have
been stories about the shyness of Meryl Streep and Bob Newhart.

The experience of being themselves in public on social occasions
is difficult for them, possibly because they work all the time and have
little interest or experience in developing a public persona. An actor
I have known for some years had the personal courage to stop a fight
outside the theater that involved a gun but faces public ceremonies
only when absolutely forced. An actress of extraordinary presence
and power describes her difficulty in accepting an acting award
before an audience in a crowded theater.

> It means that you have to get up in front of people. That's the real-
> ity. So you say, "OK, I'm doing this for the theater." In fact, I
> wanted to back out. Then I met [another actor who was also receiv-
> ing an award] . . . who was so freaked out that I thought, "He is in
> worse shape than I am," and I thought, "we have just got to go do
> this."
> When my name was called and I walked down, I thought, "All
> right, this is all the encouragement you ever wanted. Do you feel

something? No, except utter terror. Just keep walking and realize
this is what encouragement is." And I never felt it. Encouragement
comes from – I don't know what. But that didn't help.

More important to her than the public award, she decided, would be
what she could recognize as genuine praise from people she had
worked with and whose opinion she respected.

There is a difference between this protective shell that some performers create for themselves in order to deal with excessive
demands from strangers and the image projected by other kinds of
public figures. At a large political dinner in Washington, a film star
described the feeling he had that many of the politicians he met were
in danger of believing the larger-than-life personalities they generated. To him, they were what any actor would recognize as a
"role."

I think that theater people probably find the challenge of risk and
change more inviting than most people do. But the economics of the
business are usually so difficult that most of them also have to have
a very firm grip on the realities of their day to day existence.
Establishing and maintaining some basic rountine often becomes important. They have a variety of things they want from their real lives
outside work. Most want continuity, and some link between past and
present; quietude, a place to be at ease, away from stress and
competition. To many people what might be called handwork is important – carpentry, painting, constructing clothes from one's own
patterns – some mental and physical work that yields a concrete,
short-term result and gives satisfaction in skills acquired.

A orchestral conductor once said that musicians must be careful
to lead large enough lives so that they know what great music is
about. Theater people understand that as well but they struggle with
the same lack of money or lack of time as others working in the arts.
Often the bridges made by important relationships in people's lives
come about through the common experiences of caring for a family
and children. Family relationships are clearly as important to actors
as they are to actresses but women in theater seem to have more to
say about those relationships.

Actresses and Marriage – Husbands and Children

The conventional wisdom is that a married actress has an insurance policy in a husband with a regular job outside theater who

will support her while she looks for work, and that he will be pleased and proud of a wife who is part of such a glamorous profession. But acting makes demands on time and energy that at times appears excessive to nonperformers. There is an aspect of exposing oneself emotionally and physically to public scrutiny that some husbands or companions can tolerate and others can not. Actresses have both good and bad experiences with marriage. Their husbands display a variety of different attitudes towards their wives' work.

An actress who raised six children describes a husband who was cooperative and generous in helping with childcare but who didn't understand the level of commitment or discipline required by her career. Apparently, he thought of her acting as a hobby that she was pursuing for relaxation. She thought of it as a profession, although she admits that there were times when it was easier to go to the theater than it was to manage what was going on at home.

> My husband was really good about baby-sitting but he never got it into his head that it was a job or that I would need it. He expected me to go and get there at 7:30 and maybe take some people to dinner first. That was hairy. I'd sit at the [restaurant] and look at my watch and say, "I've got to get to the theater." And he'd say, "Can't you have dessert?"

An actress twice divorced and currently living in a relationship of several years, recounts a dialogue she had with her mother.

> My mother said, "I wish you would marry that man!" And I said, "But, Mother, I'm afraid. The minute I marry them, they change completely. They were all for my career and in a week, their attitude toward me changed. I've taken care of three children. All my life I've taken care of somebody else. I want to take care of me for a while. Don't you want me to be happy?"
> And she said, "No! I want you to be married."

In talking about her ex-husbands' attitudes toward her work she says

> My first husband felt a woman's place was in the home. He had been brought up that way so he felt this was a woman's job: to take care of the home, run the expenses, run the children, run parties. My second husband felt threatened by my doing something where I exposed myself so much [by performing in public]. I was married to him for a very long time. . . . . A lot of men feel threatened by women who are more successful than they, or as successful. Why should they be? If they know who they are, they shouldn't feel threatened.

Jacqueline Knapp as Lizzie and Peter Francis-James as Starbuck in
The Rainmaker by N. Richard Nash. Photographer: Joe Giannetti.
Courtesy of the Guthrie Theater.

Those men who are uncomfortable with public recognition of their wives' success are reacting to, among other perhaps more psychological strictures, a measure of status that still operates in many levels of society: that men must not appear to be less successful nor should their success be less publicly recognized than their wives'. Conversely, a man whose success is publicly recognized does not diminish the status of his wife. In fact, the recent example of Barbara Bush's being invited to speak at the commencement ceremonies of a prestigious women's college illustrates how the success of the man does not diminish but enhances the status of his wife.

Actor's wives have other difficulties in working out shared time with their husbands and rewarding lives for themselves but their status is generally enhanced and not diminished by the success of their husbands.

A recently divorced actress talks about the strains of trying to balance out several sets of obligations. Many women have the same obligations but they may not be working in as regimented and demanding a field. She brings up a crucial problem for actresses who manage families, when the job is a tour that will take them away from home for long periods. This can be particularly hard for women with children.

> I was in a marriage where a lot was demanded of me. My work in the theater was always there but the situation didn't let it take first place. I didn't let it take first place because of something in my female conditioning. I felt guilty. I lost a lot of chances because of not having that male conditioning, the drive to go ahead and take it whatever the cost.
>
> You have to be in a relationship where the other person can give you the space to do it and where you yourself can put it first, where you're not feeling compromised all the time.
>
> I had an offer to join a wonderful theater in South Africa. They tour the world. I've got two little kids. When it first came up, I thought, "Being away for a year and touring the world – it would be great! It would make my career...." As this year progresses and I look at my kids, I think, "I can't leave these guys for a year." I wonder if it would be easier for a man to do that. I feel as a mother instinctively I can't leave them. So I know I will kiss good-by to that tour.

Another actress who kept her marriage together talks about the difficulty she had resolving the tensions between her career and her personal life. She understood very clearly the cause of her difficulty but the experience was no less painful.

I'm a real classic. . . . I always had the feeling that you could not do both [family and career]. I am really a child of the time before this one. . . . I remember talking to a psychiatrist about how you could do both, but I just had this thing in my head that you were either going to have a family and get married or you were going to pursue your career. . . . I just figured I couldn't handle [both]. Or you shouldn't. It wasn't only that I couldn't handle both of them.

I think that was one reason why I admired [she mentioned another actress] so much. She has about six or seven children and she just did it all somehow. She did not have some kind of hang up that I definitely had.

The resolution of this problem of balancing career and family, aggravated by the mobility required by the profession, probably determines whether a woman stays in theater. It appears similar to a crisis point that men reach when they must decide in their mid-thirties whether or not they are making enough money to continue acting. It is a complex decision requiring an assessment of career opportunities and personal priorities. A former actress of extraordinary physical beauty talks about her reasons for restructuring her life and leaving the theater. She and her husband, also an actor, were working at the same theater when she became pregnant.

We had been married for a couple of years. I had done a number of roles. One was a very good experience. I was feeling very sensitive about any rejection in theater at that time. I wasn't as confident of my work in theater as I needed to be, of my skills. I saw my husband as much better. My ego was suffering. I couldn't see how I could continue . . . doing the kind of juggling I would have to do if I stayed. . . . Our child deserved a more stable life. I needed the order. What I was going through personally at the time propelled that. We didn't talk about it all that much. He was supportive of anything I wanted to do.

After three years at home, financial pressures sent her back to work in the business world where her present managerial position provides what she felt she missed in the theater as well as more money.

I'm very good at what I do, and that's what I needed to know. I make lots of mistakes but I feel good about myself in my role. I need the respect for what I do. Being in a small company has helped a lot. Mergers, office moves, IRS audits – I have handled a lot of that. I plan policy. I can change things. I can get people working. A lot of it's control. That's important to me.

The transition from ingenue is hard. . . . Even if women see other possibilities for themselves in character roles, directors may not. On the other hand, I sometimes think–hey, when I'm sixty-five maybe I'll go back. If you have good health and some skill, you can probably work.

This actress felt that some deficit in her own skills or talent as an actress was responsible for not being able to move into the roles she wanted. Another actress attributes these kinds of career roadblocks to certain attitudes on the part of theater management. She describes what she sees as surprisingly conventional attitudes on the part of theater administrators toward women. Maternity benefits and some job security for working women in the rest of society are reasonably common. Comparable benefits and provisions are not available for actresses. This is an area where the rest of the world is much more liberal than the theater.

> There is an extent to which you could be a giraffe and people in the theater wouldn't care. They're much more accepting of what might be considered bizarre situations but even so we still think of taking time off to have families and look for models, women who have done it and still kept their careers going without losing too much momentum.
> So I think that women do have a harder time working than men, although I hate saying that. I'd like to be more militantly sure that there is no difference. I think there is a difference in the obstacles to be overcome. There is the assumption even in resident theaters that the younger women of the theater if they are married will, of course, be having children. This is something that seems to me to feed the opinion that you're not an employee that can be counted on for a long term commitment. It's one of those unspoken questions that the government has disallowed. Somehow or other they're still there in the heads of management.

The attitude she describes is surprising since actresses and women in many other lines of work regularly carry a full workload until late in the pregnancy. In the 1960s, television performer Florence Henderson had to spend her pregnancy seated behind a high table or a potted palm because network officials assumed that viewers would be offended by having to look at a pregnant woman in a public situation. When Henderson rebelled and walked out in front of the cameras, letters poured in from the audience proving the network wrong. Thirty years later, no one thinks twice about the tastefulness of showing a pregnant talk show host on camera. Stage actresses, who have more control over their work situation, have

probably always depended on costumers to help them continue to
perform for as long as they could in a role. A 29-year-old actress who
is doing a five month tour of 35 states while she is pregnant discusses
the relative merits of her union health insurance.

> I plan to use my AFTRA health care versus my Equity. AFTRA
> covers more and there is an AFTRA office I can go to to answer my
> questions [in the Midwest]. It's very difficult trying to correspond
> with my Equity health care in New York [while on tour]. I've needed
> to fly home to make appointments with my regular doctor. I've been
> fortunate that I've remained healthy on tour. I think that this area
> should be accommodated for actors on tour, made easier, and with
> more sympathy. We're away from home and loved ones which
> makes illness or accidents more terrifying.

Her determination to make sure that she has better health care and
her expectation of more considerate treatment by unions and
theater management is quite different from sentimentalized stories
of actresses who had their babies between shows on a vaudeville
tour. She assumes that she is entitled to work and provide quality
prenatal care for herself and her child.

Those women who do work out a balance between family and
career, accomplish a very difficult way of life and talk about the
achievement with pride. Although their husbands often help, they
expect to make whatever living arrangements are necessary so that
they can do what they want to do. An actress describes her determination to work as a "passion."

When working actresses outline the organization that goes into
keeping a home running for their families, it sounds as though it
would be easier to live alone. It is common today for women to
manage both a career and a family. But most careers allow for many
free evenings and weekends, except for occasional business trips.
The theater takes up six nights a week and gives one day off, usually
Monday when the rest of the family is working or in school. An actress describes how she does this.

> When I'm working especially hard, I tend to be able to [compress]
> all my domestic duties into one and a half hours where if I'm only
> performing at night, somehow the same responsibilities become an
> eight-hour-a-day project.
> Since my husband works fulltime as well and loves his work as
> much as I love mine, our separate passions mean that we both have
> to contribute in a compacted fashion all the chores that go into

running a household. I have to have order. I can't work in chaos. Things have to be clean. There are no dishes in the sink because that's where dinner is defrosting. The freezer is full and there's an order to it that is critical to both of us being able to get off to work.

There are actors who raised their children as single parents before that phrase was invented but there are many more actresses with families who must have the organizational ability and the energy to arrange childcare and housekeeping when they work out of town. They must also have the intellectual and emotional fortitude to make these arrangements work. A woman with a young family and a very long commute talks about the concentration she finds necessary to carry what appears to be several full-time jobs.

One thing is to be very focused. Women in particular are prey to being fragmented. Someone once said the definition of being a woman is that you never get to finish a sentence. The way to get through a fragmented life is to put blinders on wherever you are at the moment. When I go to rehearsal, I have no other life. It's hard not to carry something else into an experience with you but as much as possible you have to get caught up in the moment. I think people who gravitate to theater have that – as opposed to something one cultivates. I never remember consciously working to have that but I do have it. You need that. Theater is very demanding.

An actress talks about taking a job with a theater across the country. Instead of leaving her two small daughters at home, she took them with her.

My husband would come out on weekends or every other week. I found that I had enormous energy and a very structured life. Luckily, a full-time job in theater does allow for a good bit of time with [young] children – that is, if you don't want to sleep a lot. They got up at seven, you're not called till eleven. You have a dinner break and with very young children, they're asleep at night when you're performing. So although I had sitters and playgroups for them, I still spent a great deal of time with them, and carried on a repertory of four plays.

The task of arranging for childcare in a strange city turned out to be more difficult than she first made it sound, although the theater itself and a gracious mother-in-law offered a support system.

I called an actress I know who worked there who had a daughter a year older than mine. She recommended someone to care for them.

We set it up by phone and letter. And then the night before I was to arrive, she simply called and said she couldn't. My mother-in-law said, "I'll cover for you for a couple of days." And the woman I found was better. She had children of her own and had been a Montessori teacher. And then a girl in the costume shop offered to sit in the evenings. Luck of the Irish. It worked.

To summarize, making a life outside the theater can be an important development in any performer's personal life and progress in his or her art. An older actor tells me that there are times when the discipline and craft of his art helped to solve the problems of his personal life and other times when his personal life informed and enriched what he was able to do on stage and there were other times when the two were so closely connected that he could not tell where one began and the other ended. I was impressed with his description of the interaction of life and art. I realize now, in carefully examining the difficulties of working in contemporary theater that, given the enormous energy and commitment required to pursue a career, there is relatively little time and energy left over for a life outside the theater. And therefore making a life outside the theater is a challenge. It is by most accounts rewarding but it is nevertheless a challenge. Actresses must find a partner who does not feel threatened by what they do or neglected by their separate passion. Actors must find someone who is willing to share the financial risks and the vicissitudes of change in their lives.

Much of this chapter has concentrated on the ways in which women resolve the problem of maintaining a personal life in this demanding world. All of the actresses I talked to had spent time in cultivating personal attachments outside of their careers. They were divorced, married, widowed, living with parents, children, or someone they might or might not marry. And they talked about the value of those relationships in their lives and the physical and psychological energies required to maintain them. The men I interviewed, whether or not they had cultivated or valued those relationships, spent much less time talking about them.

Actresses, although they had made the investment in husbands and children often spoke of the cost of families in terms of career opportunities lost. They often had to take into account the changes that their husbands' or companions' career dictated in their lives. Actors with families are clearly proud of being able to support them in a profession where many people cannot support themselves. But rarely did I hear from them that families or personal liaisons might cost them anything in career terms. The choices, I think, are more difficult for women. But those who work in theater may not agree.

A woman director, in thinking about her own children, suggests that it may be more difficult for actors to find women who would be willing to risk the financial instability and the vicissitudes that a life in the theater necessitates.

> I'm trying to think how I would feel as a parent if a son or a daughter said they wanted to be an actor. I think I'd probably feel the son is in for more problems, with his love life and his economic life.

There are a number of biases that operate against men who chose to work in the theater. There is so little information on cultural bias against men in the arts and particularly in theater that I think it is helpful to examine the prejudices that men feel directed against them from outside the profession. One of the stategies that men use as a bulwark against the onus they feel from this discrimination is the status, private refuge, and personal enjoyment they derive from family. Many actors feel an enormous sense of pride in being able to support a family in a field where financial stability is a recurrent problem. Actresses who function as single parents do this as well but I think they do it without the additional stress of having to prove to a skeptical world that they can.

When the Theater Is the Family

In the last weeks of August, an actress died who had worked with a particular Washington theater for 10 to 12 years. She came as an ingenue, returned after a divorce to do leading roles, and grew into one of the best character actresses the company ever had. A newspaper account gave her age as 55.

The end of the summer is generally a slow time in the theater. The company of actors she had worked with were doing workshops in Colorado. Equity houses, with the exception of Olney, run a winter season and may bring a touring show in for the summer, but their regular company members are usually out of town. Many performers use the summer to work in film or television projects – both mainly done somewhere else. Administrative staffs and actors take vacations. In brief, the end of August is a difficult time to get in touch with many people who work in theater.

Cordelia González, Margaret Medina, Akuyoe, Ivonne Coll, Natsuko Ohama, Tantoo Cardinal, Lillian Hurst, Elizabeth Fong Sung, and Laurie Souza in *Widows* by Ariel Dorfman with Tony Kushner. Photographer: Jay Thompson. Courtesy of the Mark Taper Forum.

By the second week in September most people who knew her were back in town and a memorial service was held in the cabaret room of the larger theater complex where she had worked. Probably, her last performance was in this space in a reading given earlier in the year. Arrangements for the gathering and dinner that preceded it were made by a group of friends, including the house manager whom she had asked to act as her next of kin. The Actors Fund had paid her medical bills and probably her funeral expenses. An Alcoholics Anonymous counselor who got up to speak seemed surprised and impressed with the sense that this was the actress' family, a group of people who didn't always get along with her but who accepted and understood her. And finally, they mourned and remembered her when she was gone.

Eight or nine people spoke at the service. Telegrams were read from others, directors and performers, friends who had worked with her, and her ex-husband. The head of the theater who had directed her in shows talked about her considerable talent and her ability to go beyond just the creditable performance to the extraordinary.

Another director remembered her enormous need to be reassured. She had called him a number of times at three in the morning. Three actors remembered her work, moments she had brought life to in scenes they shared, and her gritty ribald sense of humor. Most people who were there recognized her need for acceptance and her desire for closer relationships. Many of them said they felt inadequate to deal with these qualities in her personality.

The actress in the company who had shared a dressing room with her described one season of plays when the two of them and a third actress had sung and howled and laughed at the top of their lungs in the dressing room so often that the stage manager had to be sent in regularly to ask them to be quiet. They once became so raucous at a party in the theater lobby that the financial manager, ordinarily a man of unflappable calm, lost his temper and told them to shut up. In that same season, she heard the following story and shared it with the actress who died.

A man with a great sadness went to a doctor who was famous for curing depression. The doctor tried many types of therapy over a number of years. But nothing helped for very long. The man came to see the doctor so often that they became great friends. The doctor continued to look for something that would help his patient who had become his friend.

Finally, when the man came for his regular visit, the doctor greeted him in excitement, and said, "Listen! I think I have found something that will help you. There is a famous clown performing in the city. He will make you laugh, not just at what he says or does, but at what he shows you about yourself. Go and see him. His name is Grimaldi. I'm sure he will help you."

The man looked at him and said, "Doctor, I am Grimaldi."

SEVEN

BUT WHAT DO
YOU REALLY DO?

A young actor and his wife bought a house and invited some neighbors they had enjoyed meeting. The neighbors asked what he did for a living and he told them about the theater where he was working and the show he was rehearsing. They seemed very interested so he went on at some length about where he had worked before. When he stopped talking, there was an awkward pause, and then they said, "But what do you really do? How do you pay for all this? What do you do in the daytime?" To them, this was a wonderful hobby that he clearly enjoyed but it was not a serious full-time occupation and it did not sound like work.

Many of the actors I talk to have from time to time felt that people they met outside the theater discounted or devalued them because of their profession. Sometimes this takes the form of social rudeness. Sometimes it is expressed as a kind of penalty in business affairs. It may be experienced as pressure from family or close friends to give up what they are doing and chose a more appropriate career for a man. For men, disapproval of the profession is directed toward aspects of performance that appear to violate cultural norms or standards of behavior for what constitutes "serious" work.

What women may risk in choosing to make a career in theater is the cultural value of feminine vulnerability, adjusting their voice and their behavior to that of the men with whom they work. Men who choose to be actors risk never enjoying the status of men in other professions because many people do not consider acting a serious occupation for a man. It does not appear to be work. Commenting on the lack of a theater department during his years at Harvard University, an older actor says, "They had a sandbox approach to theater. It was something for people to play in."

Make-Up and Costumes

The image of the profession of theater as play in the sense that it is not serious work extends to the tools that actors use in their work, make-up, costume, and movement. A student director who keeps a foot in both worlds says, "Any man who enters the arts has to overcome societal pressures." In his experience, it is still perceived as unmanly to use make-up and dress up in costumes. "Society doesn't encourage men to use their bodies that way." Make-up is a particularly interesting example because, since stage actors have always been expected to do their own, it is an area of expertise that they must master. It is a key part of their work to study and if necessary, alter their physical features to meet the demands of a role. A characterization that has been developing in an actor's mind slowly throughout the rehearsal period, can come to life in front of the make-up mirror. When hard work and inspiration fail, make-up, costume, or eccentric movement can supply a fascinating mask to distract the audience from a thin performance. A journeyman actor lost in the existential arguments of a French play about the Trojan War said to me, "I didn't know what I was doing so I played the cloak."

Men who have spent a great deal of time in the theater may know much more about the use of make-up than women who came of age in the 1960s when the use of make-up was out of fashion. Although there are both men and women who complain of allergies, there are others who see advantages. An older character man thinks the use of cold cream and moisturizers every night have left him with younger-looking skin than men his age outside the profession.

It is common experience for young actors learning the profession to be, as someone says, "into the paint pots." Some actors continue the interest throughout their career and others decide that less is better, that change is more effectively accomplished through behavior. An actor who was himself very interested in make-up remembers a production of *The Devils*, in which he was embarrassed to watch the leading man prepare for the final scenes in the play by drawing the effects of suffering around his eyes with liner and purple eye shadow. He thought the performance would have been better accomplished with less paint and a closer reading of the script.

The size and scope of the make-up and fashion industries in this country indicate how essential the interest in youthful appearance and clothes are thought to be to women of all ages and levels of society. However, the same interest is perceived differently when it is expressed by men. Expensive lines of cosmetics have begun to be marketed for men but fashion industry studies indicate that women actually buy a larger share of these products for male friends and family members.

Physical movement as it relates to theater is another element that differentiates actors from men in the larger society. To be able to move well is an important prerequisite for an actor, but physical education for boys in this country is associated with the speed, power, and stamina of aggressive sports, not with agility and grace. During a certain period, at a local high school for boys, those who went out for football, basketball, and soccer were labelled "jocks." Those who tried out for the school shows were labelled "play fags." The pejorative nature of both labels was not taken seriously because a large number of boys did both team sports and shows. But the existence of the terms serves to illustrate a common adolescent attitude towards activities associated with two different meanings of the word *play*.

Society Can't Accept an Emotional Man

Underlying this attitude toward the outward trappings of theater is the deeper level of culturally conditioned response toward the display of emotions. An actor-director says, "For males, it's difficult because society generally can't accept an emotional man. Males are not supposed to be that way, whereas it's appropriate for a woman. Theater permits you to be open about these things."

While strong, silent, men-of-action roles have always been wonderful money makers for actors, the kinds of roles that have become the measure of an actor's talent are those that explore a character's intellectual and emotional turmoil. Lear, Macbeth, Don Juan, James Tyrone and his sons, Stanley Kowalski, Willie Loman, the fathers, sons, and brothers in Sam Shephard plays all require the exploration of a complex emotional life and the representation and

Mel Winkler as Willy Loman and Isabell Monk as Linda Loman in *Death of a Salesman* **by Arthur Miller. Photographer: Michal Daniel. Courtesy of the Guthrie Theater.**

the playing out of character flaws that lead to terrible consequences. Many of us are moved by these tragic people and we learn something about ourselves from them. But few of us, except actors, want to risk the experience of being them. In public performance, the actor explores the innermost feelings of the character, exposing private flaws and weaknesses of character. A director says,

> Men who are drawn to acting are drawn to the possibility of being able to live life in the broader emotional palette. It is a way of exploring their feelings that is safe because you don't commit the irrevocable act. The consequences of your actions are theoretical. It's an exercise in living at levels of extreme feeling which are nonthreatening.
>
> It's stressful and takes its toll on you physically almost as much as if you were living those moments in your daily life. It's a place where you're allowed to be sensitive as a male or to point out the lack of sensitivity. The literature of the theater fleshes out the male stereotype beyond what society is willing to accept or force you into. . . . It either examines the stereotype from a critical point of view or it creates new role models, unconventional, rebellious, against the tide of society. Socially defined role models of male and female are put up for examination and [can be] dismembered in the theater.

This explanation of what attracts men to the profession also describes the built-in safety net. It is possible to experience in theater the exhilaration of emotion without having to suffer the results because "the consequences of your actions are theoretical." The play exists on the level of what if, not what is. On that level, it is also possible to examine role models that have been taken for granted by both men and women and suggest other possibilities. This is relatively safe to do because the play exists in the world of ideas. But there is always some risk attached to presenting new ideas that challenge people on a very basic level. Every actor's family knows that some members of the audience can confuse a vivid performance with the man who played it. And whatever anger or negative feelings they have for the ideas of the play or the actions of a character may be directed against the performer. Added to the risk of confusing performance with performer is the observation by another director that men who continually try on other personas are suspected of not developing a mature personality of their own. There is a social stigma against men "imitating other people instead of having . . . [their] own stable identity." They are behaving too much like frivolous women who "are allowed to be more capricious."

This discussion of the actor's use of emotion again brings up the image of play, this time in the sense of not being real. "There are no irrevocable acts." Actions have only theoretical consequences. These men are only trying on other people's feelings. The director adds that recreating these actions is stressful and as physically demanding as if the experience were real. He knows and understands this because he works in the theater. He sees the work of the rehearsal process and the discipline of performance. But he is an insider. Audience members see a really good performance as effortless. They may also see it as activity that the actor enjoys, and that is another meaning of the word play.

Women in theater risk the conventional supportive, nurturing role by stepping into the aura of conflict and crafting a more powerful voice for themselves in performance. Men in theater risk violating the conventional masculine image of strength and stoicism by laying themselves open to the intellectual and the emotional life of a play in performance. They explore feelings and represent actions that may be very convincing to an audience in the moment but finally these are recognized as fictions, as having life only in the play. Men who spend their lives in the profession risk being put down as inconsequential because they have avoided the challenge of struggling

with the real business of men in the world of work. It is this world
which is a crucible for masculine identity.

Status Associated with Financial Success

All but one of the actors interviewed here had four to six years
of university education and about half came to theater with the insurance of a professional parachute. They trained to work in other
fields in the event that they could not support themselves in the
theater. Two are practicing lawyers. Other professional backgrounds
include the army, psychology, language, business, government, teaching. Most have taught in theater workshops and at the university
level. Only a small number of actresses interviewed had trained in
another field. A successful stage manager in New York recalls that
she got a degree in electronics engineering because her parents
would never have paid for an education in theater. They were per-
manently scandalized by her cousin who was an actor and, in his mid-
thirties, still couldn't pay his rent.

This nervousness about financial security in the profession affects
both sexes but creates a deeper unease for men. An actress says that
women don't expect to make a great deal of money so they worry less
about it. Another actress suggests that women may be more comfortable taking transitional jobs to support themselves until the next
acting work comes along. Wealth or financial success does not seem
to be a critical measure of status for women around the world. But
financial success has always been an important measure of a man's
status and this is particularly so in American society.

Disapproval of the financial instability of the actor's profession
could be a residual attitude from an earlier time when performers
were viewed as an underclass without the responsibilities or the
rights of ordinary citizens. There has been considerable change in
the American theater over the past 50 years as well as in the education of American actors. Drawing on the arguments of Andy Warhol,
it might even be possible to demonstrate that not only are theater
people now acceptable in middle-class society but they are actively
sought out for their status as celebrities. However, it is evident to
actors in managing their business and financial affairs that vestiges
of older attitudes survive. Mortgage loans, personal insurance, and
credit cards are still difficult to obtain for people who list acting as
their principle means of income.

Even when an actor achieves the recognizable assets of success and financial stability, he may still be subject to special scrutiny or censure. A performer who was refinancing his home in the 1980s discovered in reading the contracts that he was being required to buy high-risk mortgage insurance. Under questioning by his lawyer, the mortgage company admitted that his credit record was excellent but his profession made him a high-risk client. Another actor developed a comedy routine about applying for a housing loan at his bank, and the way he and his wife were treated by the loan officer before and after he told the man what he did for a living. A number of regional theaters have made life easier for their companies by making personal insurance accessible through board members or running informal workshops on how to apply for various types of loans, using alternative language that will not throw up a red flag to bank officials.

A related problem that has to do with the general perception of the financial instability of an actor's life is that they may be viewed as poor risks as husbands and poor providers for families. A 29-year-old actor says

> The idea is still prevalent in our society that a man must be an economic success, must be the major breadwinner in a household, and must be serious in his career pursuits ... pressures I don't think, honestly, women feel to the same extent. . . . I am currently involved in a serious relationship, and I sense a very real bias against my being an actor that I would not feel if I were a woman — the idea being that I don't have good prospects to be a provider.
>
> This pressure makes my pursuit of work in the long run more difficult. . . . Maturing as a person makes it easier for me to keep at it, and my increasing experience makes me a better actor. But my frustration at "the business" increases with age as well. Ultimately, one must learn to fall in love with the uncertainty, which makes a stable life outside the theater all the more important.

He suggests that men who do not want a conventional family life may find it easier to deal with these pressures. But other men with less conventional relationships do not agree. An actor in his mid-thirties says

> So many men drop out at a certain age because of the practical consideration that in the traditional family where the man is the bread winner, it's hard to be a bread winner when you're earning fifty dollars on stage. Also for psychological, sociological reasons, a lot

of men in my age range start to feel panicky about how little money they're making. They're not gaining societal respect because they're working in dinner theater, that they're still waiting on tables at age thirty-two.

I see more women my age who don't seem to be bothered by admitting they're not earning much money or someone is earning money for them to be [working in theater]. While I think for most men I know who, like myself, are involved in a relationship with someone who earns more money, it's a little intimidating to admit that. There's a societal pressure that says, am I being kept?

It is often assumed that the theater is a very accepting environment for gay men and women. A woman director suggests that some positions in the theater are predominantly filled by gay men. "Most critics are gay. A lot of artistic personnel are gay." But another actor makes the point that attitudes can be very different in film and television and in commercial work. This can be crucial for a performer because it is these areas of entertainment where it is possible to make a better living.

I've lived with a man for ten years. I feel that is an important part of my personality and that relationship has given me a great deal of strength. In a market like this that is relatively small, I've never actively hidden the fact that I'm gay. People over a period of time have become aware of it. But I do worry about agents becoming aware of it. People who've hired me before, would not do so again if they knew.

When I was younger, I thought it was something that would just be accepted in the theater where it wasn't elsewhere. But especially in the commercial world, in the movie world, there is a lot of homophobia. So it's sort of like if you're a woman, and you have a sensitivity about not being adequately judged by men.

Another actor in his late twenties who is getting married in a month to an actress talks about the difficulties of being able to work and stay together. They plan to try to work in the same place after they are married (New York). Failing that, they plan to try to be together wherever one of them is working. But jobs are so hard to come by that they will just have to see how things turn out. Neither will be able to afford to turn down a job. He realizes that he will have to be open to whatever they can work out.

Several actors suggest that there is a critical period for men in their mid-thirties when many of them re-examine their lives and decide whether they are satisfied with whatever level they have achieved in their career and the standard of living that it allows. Those who are not usually leave the business while they are still young enough to establish themselves in some other kind of work where they can feel more rewarded.

The threat of financial insecurity is not exaggerated. It is real but there are actors who appear to treat it as a challenge. For the men with families I have talked to, status seems to accrue from the fact that they have been able to support a family in a profession where many people can barely support themselves.

One of these men describes the special problems created by the geography of the American theater. Actors who spend a full season or more working at resident theaters where salaries are fairly substantial can make a reasonably good living, partly because of the regularity of their employment. However, there are more better paying jobs for actors in New York than in any other one area of the country. But housing in that city is more expensive and harder to find, especially if one is looking for a neighborhood in which to raise children. The actor I was talking to went to New York with a show and joined Equity. Thinking his career was launched and his money problems solved, he discovered they had just begun.

> I haven't worked in Equity since . . . we moved to New York. She [his wife] got offers there from a computer business. . . . We spent two weeks looking for an apartment . . . we got this dump for $900 a month. After two weeks of that, I said, look, let's go back to Washington. I'll try to make a career there. Let's have our kids. We'd like them to grow up near their grandparents.

For the next three years, he took a full-time job teaching and began to get film work in D.C. Cast as a principal in a recent film, he made one-quarter of his teacher's annual salary for two weeks' work.

With the increasing number of major films shot in the Washington area, actors there often find they can make far more money as members of Screen Actors Guild and the American Federation of Television and Radio Artists than they can in Equity. Movies and television projects are now shot in many different cities across the country. Both state and city governments maintain departments with a considerable staff whose function it is to attract film companies to their areas and facilitate shooting arrangements with local officials.

Although the actors quoted here are dedicated to their families and proud of them, supporting a family has been a real challenge. Another actor gives his view of what working in theater does to family life.

> The social lifestyle of theater is not conducive to people who want to sit down and relax and stay home. You've got to be willing to travel, to pack your bags and get up and go someplace. I'm only forty and I don't want to do it. I don't want to run down to Houston to do a job. I'd like to do all my work right here. I'm a homebody.

Problems are compounded by the irregular income and lack of job security.

> You get a family, you get expenses. You don't want to deal with fluctuating income. If you're in a company, you always have that problem of running into the age gap. Sooner or later this is going to be your last year with the company. It's not that you're there thirty years and you can retire and get a gold watch. It's every year, am I or am I not going to be asked back. You're vested in Equity [for pension benefits] but you might as well have a wet mattress.

Some fears are even more deeply embedded in the nature of the acting profession. Both men and women feel this but it may be stronger for men who are aware they have a family depending on them. Since men can make more money than women, they may feel a stronger obligation to do so. Someone who has been with a resident company for more than ten years voices the feeling that many actors have: that they are only as good as their last part and that they may not be able to accomplish the next one. He is talking here about how difficult the process is of creating a role.

> It's always starting over.... Criticism is harder to take.... The money is such that you can't retire. You try not to think about it. It's easy to see it as a gender problem. Most probably it isn't, but it's easy to see it as that.

A younger actor who has built a successful career, working in many different theaters, films and commercials, adds

> If you're a stock broker, you get a job with that kind of firm and then try to move up. You know which job you want next. As an actor, you don't know. I finish one job and think to myself, all right, what should I be doing now. Should I be sending out résumés? Should I be working on that audition? There's no set path.

Randall Duk Kim in the title role of Shakespeare's *Hamlet*. Photographer: Boyd Hagen. Courtesy of the Guthrie Theater.

Another beginning actor confirms this experience: "There's often no linear development." To continually work at a plan for a career under these circumstances requires a considerable amount of discipline and self-direction.

Some of these difficulties that have to do with career mobility and job security are similar to those experienced by men working in any number of industries, corporations, or small businesses in this country. Others, however, are associated with deeply felt cultural prohibitions that must be recognized if one is going to work in theater. Men do not wear make-up and dress in costume to perform the serious business of making a living. Men keep their emotions in control. They do not explain or exhibit them in public. Men who are good at their profession eventually make at least a comfortable living from it.

Actors are men who violate all of these norms. They explore, change, and use their physical appearance as a major tool in their work. They must be capable of creating and communicating a wide range of emotional life to an audience of strangers in a theater. The odds against their financial success at any age are great. Fewer than 15 percent of the members of Equity make more than a marginal living. Public perception of the glamorous lifestyle of actors is based on magazine reports of a small percentage of highly visible people.

Is There a Cultural Archetype of Masculinity?

In his 1990 cross-cultural study *Manhood in the Making: Cultural Concepts of Masculinity*,* David Gilmore finds that the answer to whether there is a "global archetype of manliness" is a "definite maybe." In most societies (not all), "manhood is a test" and there is a sliding scale of manly images and codes on which "urban Americans fall somewhere nearer the middle" range. But wherever this scale exists at all, three moral injunctions are emphasized to varying degrees. "To be a man in most ... societies ... one must impregnate women, protect dependents from danger, and provision kith and kin." Although this is a more complicated role than "the simple breadwinning mythology of Western societies," in America, definitions of masculinity are bound up with definitions of work.

*In the next several paragraphs, passages are quoted from pages 220, 222, 223, 107, 108, 110 and 49.

Manhood, as in other areas of the world, is seen as a test. Purposeful resolution and self-control are qualities that should be brought to every struggle. Giving up is less acceptable than trying and failing. Men are expected to strive hard to succeed "in the sense of profitability, getting the job done, amassing the goods" which can then be displayed in status symbols and consumer goods.

Gilmore quotes sociologists Michael Cicone and Diane Ruble who found that the "dynamic attitude about life in general with the possibility of worldly accomplishment" was pervasive in most ethnic subgroups in America. The emphasis is on material success gained through hard work and effective enterprise. There is "a parallel belief that this work ethic must be artificially inculcated in hesitant or passive males who, deep down . . . prefer not to strive." Manhood ideals force men to overcome their inherent inertia and fearfulness and to work both in the sense of expending energy and in the sense of being efficient or serviceable in doing so.

Gilmore compares the pidgin term, Big Man, used in the Pacific islands to Big Men as Americans understand them and finds many similarities. The Big Man is the richest, most successful, most competent in the group, "and he has the most of what society needs or wants. We also call powerful entrepreneurs and politicians Big Men, because they are big in the sense of power or accomplishments." The idea of the Big Man also includes a "sense of personal achievement through commanding and assertive action that adds something measurable to society's store."

Gilmore points out that these images of what it means to many people to be a man in American society recur again and again in the works of American writers from Melville to Hemingway to Philip Roth. Their stories often concern someone who is learning (or teaching) about acquiring manhood and how difficult the apprenticeship can be for a boy. It is interesting that these novelists choose to emphasize the personal challenge of manhood rather than the aspect of material acquisition.

In listening to the ways that actors talk about the forms of bias against the profession, I think a basis for negative attitudes can be found in the different meanings that theater people and those outside theater give to play and work. Bias is generally directed to the profession and only incidentally to the individual. Most actors are very good at fitting themselves comfortably into any group. Where personal relationships and friendships are involved, actors probably have the same rate of success and failure as any other group of men.

It is a response that operates against actors as part of a group that appears to place other priorities before material security and what the rest of the world can recognize as hard work.

Part of what fuels the tension between those men in the profession and those outside it has to do with the cultural tenet that men should work hard for a living and these men appear to be spending their working lives doing what is perceived by most of the world to be play. The tools of the profession, make-up, costume, movement, are serious to performers but to others are associated with play. Actors' public expression of emotion is viewed as frivolous, not manly, and it is play in the sense that it is not real. Actions have only imaginary or hypothetical consequences and the actor assumes many different personas, none of which may be his own.

Actors are getting away with doing something they enjoy for a living. They do this in spite of the fact that they may not be able to make what is perceived to be a financial success or even a continually comfortable living out of it. Given the importance of work and material success in American society, the conclusion that outsiders come to is that the profession of acting does not allow for sufficient emphasis on these two primary measures of status for men.

There are other components of masculinity enumerated by David Gilmore that are central to the lives of men who work in the theater. In most ideologies of masculinity, manhood is a test, a challenge in which a man acting on his own initiative, independent of the group, must be enterprising and effective as well as daring in his efforts to add to the security or the assets of the group to which he belongs. He must prove through his performance that he has earned the right to membership in the group. This performative aspect requires what Gilmore describes as personal autonomy, or "the underlying appeal to independent action as the starting point of manly self-identity."

Although men who are actors must face the frustration of waiting to be hired and work often in some kind of group, there are a number of ways in which every actor must be the agent of his own success. The shape of the actor's career is achieved through individual initiative and determination as well as through personal talent and luck. Even with the assistance of agents and managers, there is still no recognizable pattern for success. Most career decisions are recognizable risks in one sense or another. The economics of the profession are such that, as one actor says, it is crucial to learn how to manage one's money at whatever level of success is achieved. Competitiveness becomes habitual through continual job seeking.

Most actors have had the experience of being fired before opening. So even after getting a part, job security still depends on the actor's performance abilities.

Even small roles become an opportunity to prove oneself, to the audience, to peers, to directors, producers, to anyone with better roles to offer. Roles are also a personal challenge, a test in which the actor measures himself against his own expectations of his talent and judges whether or not he has achieved the part. This is one of the professions where men can spend all of their working lives testing and proving their abilities to themselves and their peers, and from time to time, they may feel that their talents have been recognized by the larger community and rewarded in a public manner.

For some men, there are deeper satisfactions and a larger frame of reference for what can be accomplished in the dynamic interaction between what actors and other people recognize as work and play. Someone says, "In the theater you get the feeling that you're enabling a whole group of people besides yourself to recognize the possibilities inherent in being a human being."

A Black actress gives a succinct assessment of how difficult it is to be a good actor and estimates the cost.

A really good actor is very hard to find because being a good actor ... goes against everything that the American male is. And it's hard to find somebody that brave and that smart, and acknowledge all that and still have the courage to be vulnerable.

EIGHT

ANOTHER LOOK IN THE MIRROR: FUTURE, PAST, AND PERSPECTIVE

There are performers, both men and women, who see no particular bias against women in theater. To them, the profession is difficult for everyone. There are others who see acting as a necessarily discriminatory profession. "Playwrights and screenwriters don't write to employ actors. They write to tell a story. You work in roles that you are exactly right for: age, size, sex, etc."

However, most performers generally agree that several forms of gender bias that operate against women manifest themselves clearly in the literature of theater. Most plays offer far more opportunities for men than for women. There are more roles for men and they are more significant both in terms of dramatic value and as a representation of social reality. Actors can look forward to both major and supporting roles that reach into and examine every decade of men's lives. Characterizations of women are more limited in age range and more heavily stereotyped. Roles for women are limited both in quantity and quality. Often the most productive years of women's lives are eclipsed. "At a certain age," an actress tells us, "you begin to feel invisible . . . you leap from playing the young mother to the grandmother. Where is the play that speaks to my experience of everything in between?" When so few roles portray women during those years when their life experience deepens and matures, what is suggested to both performers and audiences is that

Sab Shimono, Diane Takei, Shizuko Hoski, Jodi Long, James Saito, and Carol A. Honda in *The Wash* by Philip Kan Gotanda. Photographer: Jay Thompson. Courtesy of the Mark Taper Forum, produced in association with the Manhattan Theatre Club.

there is nothing of consequence to be found there. As the same actress points out, "Consciously or not, you begin to feel valueless after a certain age. I go to the movies and never see myself. There is no one like me. That's why I create my own work, to speak to my own experience and other women like me."

Developing New Kinds of
Theater for New Audiences

The remedy she suggests, creating another level of theater that reflects a more diverse image and addresses a segment of the audience that has been ignored, is one that women and minority groups have begun to apply in theater communities across the country. Washington has about 20 such theaters. Chicago has many more. More women are writing plays that are being produced. More men are writing plays about women. Blacks, Hispanics, and Asian-American performers are beginning to find that they have an audience that wants to understand their perspective. Some of this work eventually finds its way to the more lucrative areas of theater, film, and television. But for the most part, this is performance work that is being developed in areas of the theater where there is a limited amount of money and at a time when conservative forces have created an uneasy climate for funding of the arts. Often it is the performers, writers, and directors who subsidize productions. Those who pursue their work in these places should be able to spend some part of their professional careers earning more money in film, television, and the commercial theater. It is ironic that as this group of people develop their creative skills, the market for their respective talents and for the authenticity of the subject matter they draw from appears to be shrinking in films, television, and that part of the theater that does not have to be subsidized by the performers.

Business Decisions in the Entertainment Industry

Screen Actors Guild statistics compiled in 1987 and 1989 show a disturbing trend in that "female performers continue to work less and earn less than men in feature films, television and TV commercials" (Blake 1990, 29:12). At a recent Screen Actors Guild conference on women, keynote speaker Meryl Streep observed that when the popular entertainment business does not present images of women that young girls can recognize and admire, "the dreams of our daughters" are stifled (Streep 1990, 29:17). She suggested that the reason women are working less in the film industry is perhaps that production is dominated by adventure films which target the largely male foreign distribution market. Since two major studios, Columbia and MCA Entertainment Industries, are now owned by foreign companies, it seems reasonable to ask if this marketing strategy will be used increasingly to determine which films are produced.

In the theater, productions of serious American plays are financed through the efforts of various repertory theaters, Off Broadway producers, and the sale of television rights. Commercial producers in New York rarely mount productions of new American plays.

Nontraditional casting has been used increasingly in regional theater but rarely in Broadway productions. In the recent controversy over casting in *Miss Saigon*, newspaper reports repeatedly referred to the use of minority actors in leading roles at Joseph Papp's Public Theater and Shakespeare in the Park. None of them mentioned that the Public's financial and administrative structure is similar to resident theater. That means that performers' salaries, even for stars, are such that actors have to plan their finances carefully to be able to accept work there.

Making Better Use of the Union

One of the most useful results of the *Miss Saigon* controversy has been the initiation of a public dialogue on the difficulties faced by minority performers. Although there seems to have been some initial confusion in the negotiating strategy of the actors union, talks with the producer have produced concessions. In addition, minority union members have become more vocal in making their concerns known to union negotiators and have moved to continue the dialogue within the union. As an actor whose parents came from Lebanon and Central America points out, the economic supports and benefits enjoyed in the United States are available because working people fought for them, not because someone handed them over for the asking.

Nontraditional casting needs to be actively supported through the union to achieve any level of change in commercial theater. In resident theater, grant money provides extra incentive to theater managements and directors.

To performers, the extraordinary performance takes precedence over quite legitimate questions of ethnicity or gender. Even minority actors were reluctant to prevent Jonathan Pryce from recreating his role in *Miss Saigon* in New York. Agressive competition for roles is so much a part of the profession that the policy of making more opportunities available to minority actors and actresses probably needs to be established outside of the specific problems of the individual production.

A young white actress feels, however, that theaters "have a responsibility to enlarge the view" and addresses the dilemma that many critics raise in discussions of nontraditional casting: "An audience isn't going to accept it until it's done, but that's why it needs to be done, so that it's not an issue."

Given these difficult circumstances, it seems prudent to observe that although women and minority performers have been able to craft a voice for themselves in new areas of theater, money and the power to command it may be less accessible to these performers than it has ever been.

Access, Conditions, and Pay as Measures of Status

Actresses, like working women everywhere, make a substantial economic contribution to society. Their status, like that of other women, can be linked to access to resources (including job opportunities), working conditions (demeaning treatment of the performer or demeaning characterizations in roles that actresses are asked to play), and to material reimbursement for labor (equal pay). The estimate of worth which women, both actresses and those in the audience, draw from these measures of status has its effect on concepts of self, personhood, and autonomy for the individual. For an actress, the self-assurance that is so important in getting work can be steadily diminished by present circumstances in the profession. An actress says that as a "woman, you either have to be a doormat or such a bitch that no one can touch you. That's sort of where the circumstances lead the behavior." For women in the audience, the images that they see on the screen have little to say to them about their own experience of life. "There are many dynamic women's roles in society," says a Hispanic actor, but they "are rarely portrayed in theater. I don't know why."

These three problems, loss of roles, demeaning treatment, and inequitable pay, have been given dimension and focus through the efforts of union committees working to improve opportunities for women and minority groups. Such group support would seem particularly helpful to actresses working in isolated, temporary circumstances. Screen Actors Guild is for many performers the first of the three unions they join. It has frequently assumed a more activist role on behalf of its members than Equity. Since most performers belong to both unions, SAG's emphasis on more and better roles, equal pay, and job protection for women could encourage those who work on stage to seek more equitable terms for stage employment as well.

Although union minimums are the same for both sexes, anecdotal evidence and statistics collected by the unions indicate that women often make less money in the profession than men. With so many women entering the profession, the bargaining position is a poor one.

Mitchell Ryan as Antony and Rosalind Cash as Cleopatra in
Shakespeare's *Antony and Cleopatra*. Photographer: Chris Gulker.
Courtesy of the Los Angeles Theatre Center.

The most outspoken statement of disparity in earnings between
male and female performers comes from a report published by
Screen Actors Guild on the economic status of women members of
the union. The report, "The Female Focus: In Whose Image?" (Lateiner and Phipps 1990), is compiled from figures taken from studio
production reports on sex, age, and ethnicity. The study found that
by 1989, women members of SAG (42.6 percent) earned $296 million
while men earned $644 million. Earning power in film, television,
and theater can be directly related to who is getting the largest
number of leading roles. In 1989, the study found that female leads
were only 13.9 percent of the 49,088 roles in films and television cast
under SAG contracts. Overall the percentage of film roles for women
had dropped from 33.3 percent in 1986 to 29 percent in 1989. If these
numbers continue to drop, the future for actresses seems bleak.

The report also illustrates the disparity between the earning
power of men and women as they grow older. Earnings for men rise
dramatically in the 30–39 age group while they diminish for women.

Men in the 40–49 and 50–59 group enjoy another significant rise which diminishes only slightly in the 60–69 bracket. Women in the 40–49 group show a slight rise in earnings but their income diminishes by roughly a third in the 50–59 age group. Women in their fifties make almost two-thirds less than men in the same age group. According to this report, the only age group in which women make more money than men is in the 0–9 bracket. While there would seem to be less reason to conceal the age of children, older actresses recognize that they can lose work by giving their true age. Thus information in the report's other age categories could be skewed. Even taking this into consideration, in no age category, except the youngest, do women make as much money as men.

An older actress remembers that when she began her career, all the great stars were women. Producers make a mistake, she thinks, not to invest in the ability of women to fascinate and hold an audience. A younger actress suggests that in a time of social and economic change, men feel particularly threatened by the increasing independence and economic competition of women. They are not eager to see the position of women represented in other than conventional ways on stage and in films and television.

Another actress points to the lack of a clear path of advancement in the profession with recognizable benchmarks of success. This tends to reinforce a kind of powerlessness among performers who work from job to job. She feels this is particularly true for actresses. Even an excellent performance in a show leads nowhere if the rest of that theater season includes few plays with challenging roles. Comparing her experience in the business world, she finds that factors having to do with the itinerant nature of theater operate to preserve the status quo. Thus, those in power tend to have their position reinforced, while those with less find their position more fixed as well. It has also been her experience that the scripted view of the character portrayed tends to influence the treatment of the performer. Both of these perspectives seem to indicate more subtle layers of bias that are not addressed in discussions of gender, ethnicity, race, age or physical disability.

Regional theater can offer women better opportunities for roles and perhaps for what might be called quality of life, but it may or may not be beneficial to the shape of their careers. It is possible for an actress to make a comfortable living, work in one area long enough to keep a relationship or a family together, do plays that interest and challenge her, and acquire a broad range of skills. It is not

Trevor Jackson, Luis Ramos, Teagle F. Bougere, Roumel Reaux, David Marks, Ralph Cosham, Stanley Anderson, Henry Strozier, Kelly Chauncey Smith, and David Calloway in *Stand-Up Tragedy* by Bill Cain. Photographer: Joan Marcus. Courtesy of Arena Stage.

often possible, working in resident theater, to acquire the recognition that both feeds the soul and leads to more lucrative work. An actor who gives a brilliant performance in a new play rarely has the opportunity to recreate his performance when the play is picked up for production in New York. I think of Luis Ramos in *Stand-Up Tragedy* and Stanley Anderson in *K2*.

Actresses have even thinner prospects. Two women come to mind who did go on to New York with shows, Jane Alexander in *The Great White Hope* and Melinda Dillon, who worked with Allan Schneider at Arena Stage and then went into the first Broadway production of Albee's *Who's Afraid of Virginia Woolf*. But that was back in a time when serious American plays could still find commercial productions on Broadway.

Nurturing an Audience

An additional problem with taking resident productions to New York may be that the audience in Washington and La Jolla and Chicago and New Haven has been carefully developed and nurtured over a period of time. In these resident theaters audiences are made up of regular theatergoers who expect to give their attention to the possibilities or the problems or the questions posed by the work before them and to explore the play with the ensemble. This may no longer be true of those who make up the bulk of the New York theater audience.

Current ticket prices certainly prohibit many people from developing a habit of regular theatergoing. Subscription clubs that offer cut rate prices for plays opening on Broadway can be used by determined theatergoers. But visitors to the city rarely find these bargains. Commercial marketing techniques sell blocks of tickets to tours, corporations, conventions, and other large buyers, and these levels of bulk sales require the drawing power of major stars or a plot description calculated to entertain an audience ranging in age from 10 to 90.

Entertainment is the theater's most saleable commodity so entertainment is what must be marketed. As James O'Neill reminded his son, people come to the theater to forget about their troubles. That statement is as true of theater in New York today as it was in O'Neill's time. But if Eugene O'Neill had never written the plays he did, the American theater might still be without the towering emotional experience of authentic drama. Before O'Neill, American plays mainly consisted of melodramas in which representations of men and women were sentimentalized stereotypes.

O'Neill plays were never theater-party favorites in their own time or since, but the international reputation of American drama was established with his work. The critical examination of American culture on the stage began with his plays.

Since about 1970, fewer and fewer American plays have had commercial productions in New York. Many Pulitzer playwrights make their artistic home in regional theater. In an attempt to encourage production of more plays and to cultivate new audiences who might become regular theater patrons, theater owners and representatives of most of the theatrical unions in New York have initiated a plan for cutting production costs and reducing ticket prices.

In the summer of 1990, representatives from the theatrical community in New York put together the "Broadway Alliance: A New Plan for Play Production" (*Equity News* July-August 1990), which will extend from September 1990 to February 1992 and is subject to periodic review. The agreement will allow straight plays (not musicals) to be produced at three underused Broadway theaters at half the usual cost. Weekly minimum salaries for Equity performers will be cut by 25 percent (currently $850) and no one would make more than $2500. Ticket prices range from balcony seats at $10 to $24 for the orchestra. Concessions in salary, royalties, manpower and other costs have been agreed to by all participating groups including union technicians and the Association of Theatrical Press Agents and Managers. Those working for reduced salaries share 10 percent of any profit after the play has earned back its original investment. Run-of-the-play Equity contracts would be limited to 22 weeks. No production company will be allowed to use reduced royalty fees and salary concessions to finance a preview for a play and then transfer it to a full-salary Broadway contract. Owners of the three theaters involved are free to withdraw from the arrangement when they have the opportunity to rent the theater to producers under a full-salary contract.

One of the most encouraging aspects of this plan is that it is a move by all those who work in New York theater to accept a cut in their own profits in order to encourage new productions. This is something that performers have been doing for some time now. If reduced ticket prices do indeed bring in substantial numbers of new theatergoers, that will certainly benefit both audiences and the theater industry. But it seems reasonable to ask if those new audience members would then be able or willing to pay the regular $30 to $50 ticket prices at other Broadway theaters not participating in the Alliance. Investing in new plays and new audiences is always risky. The most lucrative forms of the entertainment industry usually work to reduce risk. Theater thrives by encouraging it.

Why Are So Many People, Particularly Women, Trying to Do This?

The harshness of these economic and personal circumstances affect everyone in the profession but present particular difficulties for women. The obvious question then is why are so many choosing theater as a career? It has probably always been true that both men and women have been attracted to the opportunities for expressiveness, the element of risk in the creative process, and the possibilities for control in mastering that process, the sense of owning the work.

As any performer knows who has struggled to get a long run and then struggled to get through it, the business has its set of difficulties for everyone. Men who choose acting as a career contend with a kind of gender bias that comes from outside the profession, as women struggle with gender bias from within the theater. Actors can experience negative sanctions expressed in public and private ways from those outside the profession who see the tools, the methodology, and the nature of performing as having little to do with hard work and not sufficiently motivated toward material success. The status of men in this country as in many others is measured by the degree of energy expended in their work and the financial success which they achieve in it. Occupations associated with the arts and unreliable incomes are acceptable for a woman but acting is not understood by many people to be a serious occupation for a man.

The rest of the world generally understands work and play as opposing terms for different activities. Theater provides a different understanding of the interaction between the two. Director Peter Brook describes how the hours of work spent in rehearsal can change in performance and become the most rewarding part of the performer's experience. "When we experience the work as play, then it is not work anymore. A play is play" (Brook 1968, 141). Actors as a group understand the interaction and the possibilities for transformation between play and work that is described here. This may be why they expect to give so much of their time and energy in a concentrated fashion to their work.

They experience both the rewards of collaborative effort in the making of a play and the exhilaration of achievement in the individual performance. There is a complicated tension between individual interest and working with the group. An actor describes the illusion of conflict created on stage in the following terms: "The people who seem to be so set against one another are really working together. But the illusion that they are working against one another is the fundamental and crucial relation." As a profession, it allows for the expression of individual autonomy and also provides opportunities for satisfaction in the approval of the group.

That every actor must be the agent of his own success is the challenge that outweighs any sanctions against the profession for many men. The individual shapes his career through his own initiative and determination as well as through the exercise of performative talent. It is a traditionally American, aggressive posture of making one's own luck. Most career decisions are recognizable risks in one way or another. Job protection is minimal. Every audition and each new role represents a test of abilities to others and to oneself. Few other professions allow for such exposure to public criticism. The economics of the profession necessitate considerable business skills in bargaining and in money management. Acting is a profession in which men can spend their lives testing and proving their abilities to themselves and their peers. From time to time they may enjoy public acclaim for having elucidated some important aspect of life for others as well.

More women are seeking autonomy, self-definition, and group status as men do, through a profession in which they find satisfaction. Women, however, may be particularly sensitive to the possibilities for transformation inherent in the nature of performance.

Three mature theater women, speaking from long, successful careers, use the image of the child learning how to command attention, sometimes with listening, sometimes with extraordinary behavior. Less restrictive processes of socialization and the availability and status of university training have made theater an attractive career option for women. University programs allow for a less abrupt initiation into the profession. Presentational skills learned and communication training can be useful to women who chose other careers as well.

An effective tool in establishing a strong sense of self comes out of the experience of performance itself. In stepping into the heightened energies generated by individual performers concentrating on their conflicting desires as the characters in the play, actresses must learn to communicate the character's demands and desires in a way that makes the playwright's intentions clear to the audience. Individual performers may be able to generate varying levels of performance energies and account for a wide variety of types of onstage presence, but all performers begin with two basic tools, language and behavior. Professional training shapes both of these as communicative devices, but it is in the continual experience of performance that they can be crafted into the kind of powerful presence that immediately establishes itself in connections between the performer, the play, and the audience. This can be a gradual learning process or a relatively rapid transformation. But it is a process that can be learned. The tools, language and behavior, are available to everyone. Training, or performance experience, can be gotten even if it is in showcases, workshops or acting classes that performers take between jobs to keep up their skills. It is in the performance experience that actresses learn to craft a more powerful voice for the characters they play as well as for themselves. "Acting is so much about conflict within a given set of circumstances," a director says. Learning to work with conflict presented in a script can be a means of conditioning women to conflict in real situations without the script. In this sense, learning to step into the aura of performance can be a tremendous opportunity for self-realization. It encourages women to craft a more powerful voice for themselves in performance and in confrontational situations in real life as well.

Everyone Wants to Be Said Yes To

As high schools in this country become larger and more impersonal, young people may look for more accessible and supportive group experience. An actress who was an only child recognized her enthusiasm for high school plays as an opportunity to be part of a larger family. "The intensity and sharing definitely was . . . not only helpful but was a large part of what drew me into it. . . . I was just ga-ga over the chance to be part of a big group that was intense and personal and exciting."

An actor says he thinks there is too much encouragement given to young people who discover the sound of applause in the school play. But an older actress believes that the desire for public approval and validation of the self may be universal to the human experience.

> We all want to be said yes to. . . . There's something in us that wants to be on stage. That's part of being human. . . . It belongs in more places than in the theater, acting. . . . I think it's a way of putting things in perspective – to make believe. It's a way of understanding that everybody wants to be applauded, a part of telling me that I'm beautiful or see me for this beautiful person, this intelligent being.

Although she understands this common desire for approval, her years of experience in the profession have made it clear to her that so much more is required of people who chose to make a career in theater.

> I wish there were more people who had something they wanted to be actors about. Why do you want to do this? What piece do you envision yourself doing? What would you like to elucidate? That's what acting is.

The Value of Theater as a Mirror for Change

In the second half of this century, the ways in which women pursue all aspects of their lives, from education to work to personal lifestyle, have changed enormously. In addition, since the 1970s, American society has become so culturally diverse that many public schools in urban areas teach English as a second language to half the children who attend them.

I think that neither of these cultural phenomena – the major changes in women's lives and the wider spectrum of ethnic groups interacting in much larger numbers in many areas of the country – is adequately represented in mainstream commercial theater, film, or television writing.

If one accepts the premise that there is a level of theater which has the obligation to examine our society as a dynamic process, then playwrights and those who write for films and television have only now begun to address the enormous changes in the lives of American women over the last 30 years.

Most women in this country now grow up expecting to work outside the home. Many women must work and raise their families without the support of well-regulated, affordable childcare. Census statistics tell us that single parent families headed by women make up the fastest growing segment of the population living at or below the poverty level. There is no longer a social stigma attached to being a "single" woman so that marriage choices are less precipitous and less irrevocable. Divorce laws have given women both more independence and less security than ever before. An increasing preoccupation with youth and physical appearance sets more rigid standards for older women than for older men.

Some of these changes appear as background noise in films and more serious television offerings. But it is in plays that the changes in society can be examined at a deeper and more immediate level of human experience. It is in plays that we begin to see a more realistic representation of ourselves and the possible consequences of the choices we make. A Black actress feels strongly that women need to see their lives validated "as much as Black people do." Another actress says

> In the work I have committed my life to, I should be able to say every once in a while, that I have been able to look at myself more deeply. Even in a large part of Black theater, I see that as Black

Leilani Jones, Freda Payne, Karole Foreman, Tonya Pinkins, and Obba Babatundé in *Jelly's Last Jam*. **Photographer: Jay Thompson. Courtesy of the Mark Taper Forum.**

playwrights try to feed more and more into the mainstream there are only certain aspects of Black life that they examine so the complexities of being a woman, of being Black, of being a Black woman are almost never examined. And you're left with having to examine aspects of life other than your own.

This is an actress speaking from the perspective of performer. She also remarks on the inevitable effect of this exclusion on the audience. If they are in the habit of going to the theater, they feel that their experience of life is somehow not important enough to be represented there. Another group never learns to go to the theater because "theater doesn't have anything to do with me. And never does. And never will." She finds this a tragic situation, for herself as performer, for those in the audience who learn to think less of themselves, and for the loss of the potential audience that might, through its expectations, become a stronger voice for change.

"Theater is a mirror of society," someone says. The paraphrase of Shakespeare's line, that plays "hold as 'twere the mirror up to nature," suggests that theater shows us, whether or not we approve the view, an eyewitness account of its own time. However, the image of the mirror is a reminder of how easy it is to see only what one chooses to see in any given reflection. If the theater has shown us a primarily male-dominated society for so many years, it did so with the acquiescence of playwrights, directors, performers, and audiences. That appeared to be a reasonably accurate representation of the world as many people saw it.

Whether or not the dominance of men in the world has changed, acceptance of that view of the world and the position of women in it has been altered by forces within society. A theater that chooses not to address the changes that all of us, playwrights, performers, directors, audiences, see around us is capable of entertaining us but it does not attempt to fulfill any of the other functions of play in our lives. It removes itself from any serious purpose and leaves us to find a locus for examining together the emotional and intellectual texture of our lives elsewhere. Finally, it becomes what a theater scholar in Moscow calls "theater from the day before yesterday."

If commercial theater, film, and television did begin to examine society with discernment, then we should see that women in real life are never limited to "the young one, the old one, and someone who's willing to play the maid." The social dialogue could be facilitated not only between men and women but also between traditional theater and those Americans who until now have had only muted voices and supporting roles.

Taking issue with some nontraditional casting choices in a production in Washington, one critic cited population statistics for the state of New Hampshire in 1910 and for the present time. This literal-minded argument would seem to ignore the ability of the creative work to represent a specific time and place and at the same time to evoke for its audience other times and other places that give the events of the play significant meaning for them. A play, however real it may seem, exists only in an imaginary time and place which may be manipulated in any number of ways by the author, the director, the performers, or the audience. Time may be a metaphor for the future. It may refer to past experience, or it may signify a continuing now.

In Oni Faida Lampley's play, *Mixed Babies*, a group of Black girls having a slumber party in the 1950s gasp at an obscenity and disapprove of divorce, features that root them firmly in that time. But the prologue to the play alludes to initiation rites that celebrate ancient resources of strength. Finally, the play ends with a mixture of irony and hope that speaks to the individual's experience of ritual and ceremony without reference to time or place.

Reality in the theater consists of illusions that must appear to be real. Credence in those illusions depends both on performance and the limits of imagination in the audience. The tension that exists between those two changing entities can be a nightly challenge for the performer. "You walk out into this space and anything can happen."

If the theater, as many critics have said, is the most accessible of the arts, then perhaps the theater is also the most effective of the arts in its ability to reexamine our vision of social reality. A number of theories in cognitive anthropology and sociolinguistics suggest that social reality consists in negotiated interactions of individual perceptions of events. Together we compare our perceptions and negotiate the meaning of what we see happening in the world around us. The theater as a communal experience seems admirably suited to this kind of negotiation of meaning.

A Black actress reaffirms the larger value she finds in working in this difficult, rewarding profession.

> Communicating something you've discovered. Putting life in perspective. The arts help to do that. They tell us what's happening in the world. They figure out concepts and perspectives. They do futures. They analyze the past. They put things in perspective.
>
> The more informed they are, the more effective they are as communicators and artists whether [those who work in the arts] be painters or actors or singers. Because you bring more than the note you sing and the instrument through which the notes come, [you bring] an understanding of something that's not tangible.
>
> I have an idea that if a lot of people would delve into what it takes to be an actor, it would change their lives.

BIBLIOGRAPHY

Agar, Michael H. *Speaking of Ethnography.* Sage University Paper Series. Beverly Hills, Calif.: Sage Publications, 1985.

Blake, Timothy. "Are Women All Washed Up at 40?" *Screen Actor,* fall 1987, 18–19.

Brook, Peter. *The Empty Space.* New York: Atheneum, 1969.

Chinoy, Helen Krich, and Linda Walsh Jenkins, eds. *Women in American Theatre.* 2nd ed. New York: Theatre Communications Group, 1987.

Clifford, James, and George E. Marcus. *Writing Culture: The Poetics and Politics of Ethnography.* Berkeley: University of California Press, 1986.

Espinosa, Theodore Paul. "Text-Building in a Hollywood Television Series: An Ethnographic Study," Ph.D. dissertation, Stanford University, 1982.

Equity News. March, December 1988; November, December 1990; January, March, April 1991.

Gilmore, David D. *Manhood in the Making: Cultural Concepts of Masculinity.* New Haven: Yale University Press, 1990.

Houston, Velina. "It's Time to Overcome the Legacy of Racism in Theater." *Los Angeles Times,* 13 August 1990, F3.

Lateiner, Roger, and Tony Phipps. "The Female in Focus: In Whose Image?" *Screen Actor,* fall 1990, 12–13.

Mamet, David. *Writing in Restaurants.* New York: Viking, 1986.

Mekler, Eva. *The New Generation of Acting Teachers.* New York: Penguin Books, 1987.

Moore, Henrietta L. *Feminism and Anthropology.* Minneapolis: University of Minnesota Press, 1988.

Pace, Guy. American Equity Association. 30 March 1987. New York. Personal communication.

Schechner, Richard. *Between Theater and Anthropology.* Philadelphia: University of Pennsylvania Press, 1985.

Shapiro, Laura. "Where Are All the Men?" *Newsweek,* 10 April 1989, 62–63.

Stewart, Charles J., and William B. Cash, Jr. *Interviewing Principles and Practices.* 4th ed. Dubuque, Iowa: Wm. C. Brown, 1985.

Streep, Meryl. "When Women Were in the Movies," *Screen Actor,* fall 1990, 15–17.

Turner, Victor. *The Anthropology of Performance.* New York: PAJ Publications, 1986.

Viola, Tom. "Equity Employment: A Recent Update." *Equity News,* February 1987.

Woolf, Virginia. *A Room of One's Own.* New York: Harcourt, Brace, 1929.

INDEX

Actors' Equity Association 14, 18,
    31, 33, 35, 42–43, 47, 78, 80,
    84–86, 90–99, 105, 115, 118, 129,
    130, 132, 141, 145–146
Actors Fund 119
Addams, Jane 14
Adler, Stella 77
AFL-CIO 92, 100
AFTRA *see* American Federation
    of Television and Radio Artists
age bias viii, ix, xi, 1, 6, 20–25,
    42, 81, 130, 137–138, 142–143,
    150
Ahmanson Theater 18
Albee, Edward 144
Alcoholics Anonymous 119
Alexander, Jane 144
American Federation of Television
    and Radio Artists 90–91, 97,
    115, 129
American realism 77
Anderson, Stanley 144
anthropology vii, viii, x, xi, 5, 29,
    89–90, 132–135, 147, 153
*The Anthropology of
    Performance* vii
Arena Stage xii, 13, 94, 144
Arsenic and Old Lace xii, 6
As You Like It 18
Association of Theatrical
    Press Agents and Managers 146

Baltimore-Washington 87
Barry, Philip 4

Blake, Timothy 43
Brecht, Bertolt 16
Broadway xi, 13–14, 18, 22, 30,
    61, 75, 93, 98, 100, 139, 144,
    146
Broadway Alliance: A New Plan
    for Play Production 145
Brook, Peter vii, 147
Bush, Barbara 112
business of theater viii, xi, xii,
    4–6, 11, 13, 29–35, 40, 42–43,
    77–101, 109, 118, 127–130,
    132, 139–140, 142, 145–148,
    152

CBS 12
Center Theater Group 18
Chekhov, Anton 14
Chicago, Illinois x, xii, 11, 14, 138,
    144
Chinoy, Helen Krich 14
Cicone, Michael 133
Cleopatra (role) 18
Colorado 118
Columbia Pictures 139
Comden, Betty 2
Cooper, Gary 23
Cordelia (role) 26
Cornell, Katharine 2, 65
The Country Girl 54
Coward, Noel 4
Cowl, Jane 2
Crawford, Joan 23
Crimes of the Heart 16

157

Davis, Bette 23
Denver x
The Devils 122
Devil's Disciple 6
Dillon, Melinda 144
Don Juan (role) 123
Dramatists Guild 2
Duke University 13
"Dynasty" 23

The Empty Space vii
Equity *see* Actors' Equity
    Association
Equity News xi, 6, 145
Espinosa, Paul xi

"Falcon Crest" 23
Falstaff (role) 21
"Female Focus: In Whose
    Image?" 142
Fichandler, Zelda 13, 14
film ix, x, xi, xii, 5, 11, 19–20,
    22–23, 26, 30, 42–43, 56, 61–63,
    78–79, 86–88, 97–98, 100, 105,
    107–109, 118, 128–130, 139,
    142–143, 150, 152
Ford Foundation 94–95

Gabler, Hedda (role) 95
Georgie (role) 54
Gertrude (role) 32–33
Gilmore, David 132–134
The Glass Menagerie 18
Glengary Glen Ross 73
Goetz, Ruth 2
Goodman School 11
Goodman Theater 18
The Great White Hope 144
Grimaldi 120
Group Theater 77

Hamlet 32–33
Hamlet (role) 26

Hanna, Judith vii
Hansberry, Lorraine 18
Harvard University 122
Hayes, Helen 2
Hedda Gabler 56
Hemingway, Ernest 133
Henderson, Florence 114
Hepburn, Audrey 23
Hollywood, California 25
Houston, Velina 99
Houston, Texas 130
Hull House 14
Huntington Theatre Center 18

Jenkins, Linda Walsh 14
Jersey City, New Jersey 19, 92
Jones, Margo 14
Juliet (role) 24–26, 81
Juno and the Paycock 6

K2 144
Kaufman and Hart 16
Kennedy Center 36
King John 26

La Jolla, California 144
Lady Bracknell (role) 21
Lady Macbeth (role) 18
Lampley, Oni Faida 153
Lateiner, Roger 142
Lavinia (role) 67–68
Leacock, Eleanor 29
League of Regional Theaters x,
    14–15, 18, 30, 78, 94–95, 97
League of Washington
    Theaters 18
Lear (role) 26, 53, 123
Loman, Willie (role) 123
Look Back in Anger 4
LORT *see* League of Regional
    Theaters
Los Angeles, California 88, 94,
    100
Los Angeles Times 99

lower pay for women 29–35,
    40–43, 139, 141–142, 146

Macbeth (role) 123
McKellen, Ian 24
Mamet, David xii, 77, 79, 88–89
Manhood in the Making 132
The Marriage of Bette and Boo 18
MCA Entertainment Indus-
    tries 139
Meisner, Sanford 77
Melville, Herman 133
Miranda (role) 18
Miss Saigon 98–99, 139–140
Mistress Quickly (role) 21
Mixed Babies 153
Molière 14
Moore, Henrietta viii, 29
Moscow 152

National Theater xii
Neighborhood Playhouse 77
New Haven, Connecticut 144
New York vii, x, xii, 2, 6, 12–18,
    31, 36, 57, 62, 73, 75, 83–85, 88,
    90–95, 97, 100, 126, 128–130,
    139–140, 144–146
New York City Commission on
    Human Rights 100
New York Times 14, 98
Newhart, Bob 108
'night Mother 16
Nin, Anais 66
non–Equity theaters 92–93
nontraditional casting viii, 5–6,
    17–21, 27, 98, 100, 139–142,
    150–152
NYU 13

Off Broadway 18, 139
Old Globe Theater 18
Olivier, Laurence 52

Olney Theater 118
O'Neill, Eugene 145
O'Neill, James 145
O'Neill Center 18
Osborne, John 4
owning the work 61, 65–75, 146

Papp, Joseph 140
Paulina (role) 18
PBS 18
Pennsylvania 19
Phipps, Tony 142
The Piano Lesson 18
*The Playboy of the Western
    World* 18
Prosky, Robert xii, 103, 106
Pryce, Jonathan 99, 140
Public Theater 140
Puck (role) 21
Pulitzer 145

Quakers 64

Raisin in the Sun 18–19
Ramos, Luis 144
regional theater x, xi, xii, 1, 7, 11,
    13–17, 21–22, 32, 46, 50, 53, 58,
    62–63, 65, 69, 77, 80, 86, 93–97,
    100, 114, 118, 127, 129–130, 138,
    140, 143–145
resident theater *see* regional
    theater
Rich, Frank 14
Romeo and Juliet 81
Rosalind (role) 18
Roth, Philip 133
Ruble, Diane 133

SAG *see* Screen Actors Guild
San Francisco, California x
Schechner, Richard vii

Schneider, Allan 144
Screen Actor 42
Screen Actors Guild 42–43, 78,
    90–91, 97, 129, 139, 141–142
sexual harassment 29–30, 36–43
Shakespeare 1, 14, 16, 21, 24–27,
    32, 56, 67, 81, 140, 152
Shakespeare in the Park 140
Shaw, George Bernard 14, 53
Shepard, Sam 16, 123
Sherwood, Robert 4
small theater production con-
    tract 31, 78, 92–93
Spanish 69
Stand-up Tragedy 144
Stanislavski 77
Stanley Kowalski (role) 123
stepping into the aura 10–11, 41,
    45–60, 125, 149
STP *see* small theater production
    contract
Strasberg, Lee 77
Streep, Meryl 108, 139

Tamara (role) 32–33, 67–68
television ix, xi, xii, 5, 11–12,
    18–20, 23, 26, 30–31, 42, 61–62,
    65, 78–79, 81, 87–88, 90, 97,
    100, 105, 108, 114, 118, 128–130,
    139, 142–143, 150, 152
The Tempest 6, 18
Tennessee x

Titus (role) 67–68
Titus Andronicus 32–34, 67–68
Trojan War 122
Turner, Victor vii
Tyrone, James (role) 123

United States vii
university theater 12–14, 47–48,
    77, 122, 148

Vance, Nina 14

Warhol, Andy 126
Washington, D.C. viii, ix, x, xi,
    xii, 6, 13, 15, 17–18, 43, 69, 91,
    109, 118, 129, 138, 144, 152
Wasserstein, Wendy 2
*Who's Afraid of Virginia
    Woolf?* 14
Wilson, August 18
The Winter's Tale 18
Woolf, Virginia 24
Writing in Restaurants 88

Yale Drama School 13
Yale Repertory Theater 13, 18